Arata Isozaki

Arata Isozaki

FOUR DECADES OF ARCHITECTURE

Richard Koshalek • *David B. Stewart*

THAMES AND HUDSON

First published in Great Britain in 1998 by Thames
and Hudson Ltd, London

British Library Cataloguing-in-Publication Data
A catalogue record for this book is available from
the British Library

ISBN 0-500-28088-6

Printed in Italy

CONTENTS

Preface by Richard Koshalek 7

"Irony and Its Fulfillment" by David B. Stewart 12

CITY IN THE AIR 26
Shinjuku Project (Joint-Core System)

1960s: System 30
by Arata Isozaki

1970s: Metaphor 70
by Arata Isozaki

1980s: Narrative 112
by Arata Isozaki

1990s: Form 158
by Arata Isozaki

Preface

Arata Isozaki is one of the most innovative and influential architects working today.
Over the last four decades, he has designed an extraordinary series of projects and
buildings that have made a significant contribution to the evolution of contemporary
architecture worldwide. His highly original approach replaces the purely rationalist
precept underlying modern architecture with a more personal, even idiosyncratic,
aesthetic—one that is a synthesis of historical symbolism and the most advanced
developments in technology and communication. His architecture neither blatantly
quotes from a romantic past nor wholly embraces the hyper-technology of the present,
but rather creates a delicate balance between these forces in a specific contemporary
context.

In the summer of 1980, Isozaki began to work with The Museum of
Contemporary Art, Los Angeles, on the design of its California Plaza structure. The
museum was Isozaki's first major commission in the United States and, as such,
marked a particularly crucial point in his career. Since its completion in 1986, MOCA
has received resounding acclaim throughout the world, bringing continual attention
to an architect of exceptional sensibilities and supreme talent.

With the celebrated inaugural exhibition of the museum in 1986, the MOCA staff
was again privileged to collaborate with Isozaki on the California Plaza installation
design of "Individuals: A Selected History of Contemporary Art, 1945–1986." Since
that time, we have worked with the architect on additional designs for two exhibitions:
the Louis I. Kahn retrospective organized by MOCA for an international tour that com-
menced at the Philadelphia Museum of Art in October 1991, and the exhibition examining Isozaki's own remarkable career that is documented in this revised catalogue. In
addition, through the generosity of the Laura-Lee Whittier Woods Foundation, in 1997
the museum again collaborated with Isozaki in realizing his original 1986 design for
the canopy covering the entrance courtyard.

The museum was profoundly honored to have presented the retrospective of
Isozaki's work, timed to coincide with his sixtieth birthday, an occasion that has spe-

cial significance in Japanese culture. According to Japanese legend, by age sixty an individual has accumulated sufficient experience to have achieved the essential wisdom and knowledge necessary to make significant contributions in the future. *Arata Isozaki: Architecture 1960–1990* was a thorough examination spanning thirty years of the architect's impressive œuvre, from the early visionary proposals of the 1960s to the large-scale urban projects of the present. The exhibition both illuminated the complex, multifaceted nature of Isozaki's past work and provided insights into directions that the architect may pursue in the future. Documenting more than thirty projects and buildings, the exhibition included a full-scale "folly" reconstruction at MOCA, as well as forty scale models, 250 original drawings, and a series of three high-definition television presentations, each focusing on a different phase in Isozaki's career.

The architect's work was installed in five thematic groups. "Theme I: Genesis of Imagination" featured conceptual proposals for Tokyo from the 1960s, including such schemes as Clusters in the Air and the Marunouchi Project, along with such high-tech environmental designs as the Computer-Aided City. These projects demonstrated Isozaki's early interest in merging technology with urban design, and showed an already rich imagination working to address the challenges of contemporary urban existence.

The evolution of Isozaki's work over the following decades was explored in three successive phases, beginning with "Theme II: Birth of an Architect." This section, which focused on the early concrete buildings and those public structures of bold geometric form realized primarily on Isozaki's home island of Kyushu, examined his emergence as a rising architect. These designs include the Fukuoka City Bank Head Office; the Fujimi Country Clubhouse; the Kita-kyushu City Museum of Art; the Kita-kyushu Central Library; and the West Japan General Exhibition Center. "Theme III: Catastrophe Japan" explored Isozaki's search for a more individual architectural expression, one that also incorporated references to past historical styles. Among the buildings included in this period (to which the term "schizophrenic eclecticism" has been applied) are the Gunma Prefectural Museum of Fine Arts; the Kamioka Town Hall; the Tsukuba Center Building; and the Art Tower Mito. "Theme IV: Architect as World Citizen" included the Phoenix Municipal Government Center; The Museum of Contemporary Art, Los Angeles; the Brooklyn Museum; the Sant Jordi Sports Hall; and several other international projects that occupied Isozaki in the latter part of the 1980s.

The exhibition concluded with "Theme V: Hyper-Technology," comprising Isozaki's proposals for the Tokyo City Hall, Ueno Station, and the NTV Plaza redevelopment plan. These projects presented his mature thoughts for a greatly changed Tokyo in the 1990s, three decades after the initial proposals shown in "Theme I" of the exhibition. In this way, then, the exhibition came full circle through the fascinating terrain of the architect's brilliant and highly charged imagination.

In the years since the exhibition, Isozaki's contribution to architecture has grown, as demonstrated by the projects included in this revised edition. The major commissions of the 1990s, including the Toyonokuni Libraries for Cultural Resources, the Nara Convention Hall, and the Center of Science and Industry in Columbus, Ohio, reveal an architect who challenges the conventional definition of form.

The exhibition and this book resulted from the exceptional cooperation and dedication of Arata Isozaki and his wife, Aiko Miyawaki. They devoted an enormous amount of time, energy, and creativity to this collaboration, for which we remain exceedingly grateful. Their inspiring work has been a vital and compelling force abetting us throughout our endeavors. The supremely committed and efficient staff of Arata Isozaki and Associates, including Hiroshi Aoki, Yoshiko Amiya, David Gauld, Ko Ono, Tomoko Mizukami, and Shuichi Fujie, contributed immeasurably to the realization of the exhibition, and we express our continuing appreciation to them for their extraordinary care and assistance. I would also like to recognize and thank my co-curators, François Burkhardt, former Director of the Centre de Création Industrielle, Centre Georges Pompidou, now current editor of Domus, and Akira Asada, Associate Professor, University of Kyoto, for their invaluable participation in this project.

I am deeply grateful to the Board of Trustees of The Museum of Contemporary Art and its Program Committee for their recognition of the importance of architecture and design as an essential component of a balanced museum program that reflects the reality of contemporary culture. Our special gratitude goes to Frederick M. Nicholas, former Chairman of the Board of Trustees, Audrey M. Irmas, the present Chair, and Lenore S. Greenberg, Program Liaison, for their leadership, support, and keen sensitivity to the museum's programming concerns and for their ongoing encouragement of the curatorial staff.

I would also like to thank those staff members of The Museum of Contemporary Art who worked closely with me on this project. Special recognition is due to Sherri Geldin, currently Director of the Wexner Center for the Arts, who played an integral role at every phase of this project, from the early conceptual stage through the many creative and logistical planning sessions that occurred over several years. She and Bonnie Born, executive assistant, traveled with me to Japan at the invitation of Arata Isozaki and Asahi Shimbun to help organize the exhibition and arrange for its premiere in Los Angeles. An important contribution was also made by MOCA Assistant Curator Alma Ruiz, who became involved in the project at an important stage in its organization and presentation in Los Angeles.

9

Particular thanks go to other members of the staff as well, among them former Editor Catherine Gudis, who worked closely with Rizzoli International Publications to produce the original edition of this book; current Editor and Associate Curator Russell Ferguson, who collaborated on this revised edition; and Director of Development Erica Clark, who provided the leadership necessary to obtain appropriate funding for this project's presentation in Los Angeles, and also provided editorial expertise. We are also grateful to Exhibitions Production Manager John Bowsher and his outstanding staff for their work on the installation and, particularly, for their fabrication of the full-scale "folly"; to former Registrar Mo Shannon, who assisted our colleagues in Japan with all shipping and registration; and to Chief Financial Officer Jack Wiant, who provided financial and administrative assistance.

My profound thanks to Yasuhiro Ishimoto for his superb photography and, especially, to David Stewart, architectural historian and Visiting Foreign Professor at Tokyo Institute of Technology, whose special insights into Isozaki's work are of inestimable value. Special mention is also due to Elizabeth Johnson and Charles Miers at Universe Publishing for their critical contribution to this revised and newly formatted edition.

The exhibition was organized by The Museum of Contemporary Art, Los Angeles; the Centre de Création Industrielle, Centre Georges Pompidou, Paris; and the Asahi Shimbun, Tokyo. Generous support was provided by the East Japan Railway Company and the Fukuoka Culture Foundation/Fukuoka City Group in collaboration with Matsushita Electrical Industrial Co., Ltd. These institutions have our continuing gratitude for their essential collaboration and their magnificent encouragement of this endeavor from its inception.

Following its opening in Los Angeles, the exhibition travelled to twenty museums throughout the world.

The republication of this book is a further testament to Arata Isozaki's achievements, and we wish the greatest ongoing success in this remarkable career. His intellectual, spiritual, and creative energies have immeasurably enhanced and enlivened the critical international dialogue within the world of architecture and urban design, and far beyond as well.

RICHARD KOSHALEK, *Director*
The Museum of Contemporary Art, Los Angeles
May 1998

For the first twenty years of my career, I believed that architecture could only be accomplished through irony.

. . .

It could allude to treason.
It could be criticism.
It could champion the vulgar against the noble, the secular against the sacred, without shame.

. . .

It was an unfulfilled wish, a mourning for what was lost—
Hiroshima, holocaust.
To bridge over the gap—
Wit, a sense of humor, and paradox were called for.

. . .

Now, after twenty years of hands-on experience, I am going to find a way of making architecture without irony.

ARATA ISOZAKI, "Architecture With or Without Irony," 1985

Irony and Its Fulfillment

DAVID B. STEWART

The perspective view of Isozaki's submission for the 1980 Tegel Harbor competition in Berlin was freely adapted from Plate 115 of Karl Friedrich Schinkel's *Collection of Architectural Designs*, which depicts the Berlin Building Academy, finished by Schinkel in 1836. The engraving by Mandel, after Schinkel, published in 1833—a year after the Building Academy was begun—is the last of the great architect's much-loved topographical views drawn from the banks of the River Spree. Like the Tegel Harbor Complex, the Building Academy project was conceived in a spirit of urban improvement, and Schinkel actually lists the advantages that "will come about as a natural consequence of this project." The school itself occupies the former site of a customs depot, and its planning suggests various street widenings, the provision of new amenities, and the disengagement of urban vistas, none of which Schinkel wishes to have escape public notice.

Still, despite the fact that the ensemble of Schinkel's works, such as were built, profoundly changed the face of Berlin in the course of the architect's lifetime, he was never allowed free rein of his instinct as an urban planner. Instead of being called upon by his sovereign to redesign whole districts of Berlin, the Prussian capital—or even isolated spatial tracts—Schinkel was, even as state architect, obliged to live by his wits. Fortunately, he built widely enough within the city that his works do coalesce, leaving Berlin with his inevitable stamp—just as Isozaki's three major buildings in Kita-kyushu City endow that town with an architectural character rare in modern-day Japan.

Isozaki's Tegel project, however, remains unbuilt, like so many of Schinkel's refinements, not to mention the Berlin master plan of 1817. The waterfront design Isozaki elaborated in 1980 transforms the footprint of the now vanished Building Academy into a skewed open plaza. This is partially colonnaded and presided over at its center by a "dummy facade" replicating Schinkel's Humboldt-Schloss in Tegel, with steps leading away obliquely in the corner opposite, down the embankment to the water.

As is well known, Schinkel's engraved drawings are stripped to a bare formal minimum. In fact, for us today this constitutes the essence of Schinkelian neoclassicism. Thus, too, the famous Berlin monuments—the museum, the theater, and the Building Academy—are models of architectural clarity and restraint, works created when Schinkel was at the pinnacle of fame and favor. But, earlier, he had turned to the elaboration of panoramas, a new, light-based medium that first appeared in Berlin in 1800. Schinkel's initial essay in the technique was an 1808 view of Palermo, of which only an engraving survives but which must have been exhibited fully in the round, with no side edges—the beginning connected to the end—and illuminated by means of a high, hidden light source.

There were few lapses of scenographic interest in designs of this sort. The same shoulder-to-shoulder jostling of built forms characterized Schinkel's work for the

Karl Friedrich Schinkel. Project for a Royal Palace on the Acropolis, Athens, 1834.

stage, which continued well into the 1820s, in particular his Egyptianized sets of 1815–16 for Mozart's *Magic Flute*. Likewise, an extremely complex romanticism, both functional and ideological, surfaces continually in Schinkel's numerous unbuilt palace designs of the 1830s. These take their inspiration from Pliny's villa, a reconstruction of which was intended at Charlottenhof for the Crown Prince Friedrich Wilhelm. Schinkel's *Collection of Architectural Designs* ends with a later version of this scheme. Perhaps even closer to Schinkel's own inclinations were plans for a Crimean palace overlooking the sea near Yalta, to be inhabited by the Czarina, Friedrich Wilhelm's sister. While the elevations, apart from the siting of the palace itself, are unremarkable, the polychromic interiors in an "Asiatic-Scythian" style and the hanging gardens would have created the most elaborate scheme of Schinkel's career. In terms of complexity of organization and massing, the so-called Ideal Capital City (or Residence of a Prince) remains Schinkel's most ambitious design.

Most striking of all these late schemes was Schinkel's redevelopment of the

Acropolis at Athens as a royal palace for Otto of Greece. This is again a coloristic exercise, under the influence of current research into the appearance of classical architecture. The palace itself would have been discreetly sited to the rear of the Parthenon and Erechtheion. In the magnificent colored lithographs of these two projects, for Athens and the Crimea, published toward the end of Schinkel's life and posthumously, the picturesque is raised to a new level and scale.

In this eventual pilgrimage to the Acropolis we have come a long way from the Tegel Harbor Complex entry of 1980, as well as from the built œuvre of Schinkel himself. Yet, just one year before his death in 1841, Schinkel is recorded as discussing the re-exhibition of the Palermo panorama. Moreover, Schinkel raised a new idea for the public exhibition of a panoramic display of monuments, from ancient Egypt and Greece down to medieval Germany. Together with the last projects described above,

Arata Isozaki. Competition entry for the Tegel Harbor Complex, Berlin, 1980.

the trend of such grandiose historicizing is once more as clear as it may seem to us today inevitable. For his part, Isozaki developed his Tegel scheme of 1980 in the very year following James Stirling's Shinkenchiku Residential Design Competition, whose given theme was "A House for Karl Friedrich Schinkel" (*Japan Architect*, no. 262, February 1979), and the year preceding the bicentennial of Schinkel's birth. K. F. Schinkel stood revealed as the man of the hour.

What, then, were the conditions of genius, and historical inevitability, that led Arata Isozaki to a postmodern historicism? It goes without saying that they were as unique to the Japan of the Showa era as those governing the meteoric ascent of Schinkel were to the Prussia of Friedrich Wilhelm III. We have sought to recall some of the ways in which the great Prussian architect prefigured the professional of the twentieth century, but we must also recall how in the late spring and early summer of 1804, Friedrich von Schiller visited Berlin and Potsdam in contemplation of a permanent move there from Weimar. Schinkel had left Rome and spent that summer traveling in Sicily, considering the landscape and temples and sketching, to be sure. By March 1805, Schinkel was back in Berlin; by May of the same year, Schiller, having remained after all at Weimar, was dead.

Culturally, Schiller's disappearance marks a watershed, one that, together with the French Revolution and Napoleon's ascent, helped define the romantic classicism of the period, of which Schinkel was a decisive, if late, representative.

But whereas neoclassicism as a "style" engendered innumerable instances of artistic devaluation, not least in the years of the Empire—a time when heroic themes were frequently translated into drawing-room bric-a-brac—Schiller's pivotal role, in his partnership with Goethe, and also the brevity of his career seem to have precluded triviality. He had little enough to do with architecture and was concerned even less than Goethe with any form of antique revival in visual terms. His importance lies in the fact that in the Germany of his time, barely emerged from its feudal past into the modern era, Schiller's access to meaning was through history. And this meant universal, or world, history, for Schiller discovered his models in Gibbon, Herder, and Kant. From the beginning his dramas and essays aimed at nothing less than a historical understanding of the revolutionary present. It was, moreover, a significant feature of Weimar classicism that aesthetic comprehension served to provide moral guideposts for a future society. In terms of architecture, the modern movement was the grateful inheritor of these notions, and Schinkel, who was fifty-one at the time of Goethe's death, was instrumental in conveying this ethos in built form to the early twentieth century.

The exemplar of Weimar classicism propounded by Schinkel at a truly civic scale reached Japan through the country's experience of modern architecture and, more especially, of the International Style. Following the Meiji Restoration of 1868 Japanese nation-builders were widely receptive to Prussian innovations of their day, including the bombastic Bismarckian German Renaissance style. Indeed, that very degeneration from Schinkel's standards of restraint and purity offered the raison d'être for the first "rediscovery" of Schinkel's style. The Loos-Behrens-Mies connection of the early twentieth century saw to it that Schinkelian example, as canon, was absorbed and reiterated in a "modern," radically dehistoricized version (no Royal Palace on the Acropolis, for example). Such was the condition imposed eventually also in America, not to mention Japan and elsewhere. Yet the question still is asked whether the cold and beautiful abstract formalist architecture of European modernism merited its universal application.

Initially, we need to remember that not until 1868 did Japan become a modern political entity, and the story begins, from scratch, yet again in 1945. By the latter date,

Japan had received the flame of modern architecture, albeit by that time most of her not inconsiderable examples were literally in flames—or in ruins. Tokyo and other cities, most infamously Hiroshima and Nagasaki, were not even that. So the question of architecture, of building, was posed anew in critical terms. In the capital, a few buildings, mostly large and well constucted, did not succumb: the Imperial Diet Building, the Tokyo Central Post Office, Wright's Imperial Hotel, the Marunouchi office building, Dai-Ichi Insurance (later to be the American G.H.Q.), much of the Imperial University, the Bank of Japan, Meiji Insurance, various schools and hospitals, the prime minister's official residence, some public housing, Honganji Temple, and others. Mostly they were works of the 1920s and 1930s, including occasional masterpieces, such as Tetsuro Yoshida's post office; some iconic but ideologically sullied monuments, such as the Imperial Diet; and some notable landmarks in Western revival styles, like Tokyo Station and the Bank of Japan.

Evidently, too, the reconstruction of damaged cities had received consideration. Before the war's end, young Kenzo Tange had devised a program of "three-dimensional urban design." In practical terms, this comprised a survey of areas most likely to be bombed, research in the university library on the Greek agora and Roman forum, and participation in government-sponsored design competitions, such as the Japanese Cultural Center in Bangkok (1943) and the Greater East Asia Coprosperity Sphere Memorial near Mt. Fuji (1942). Tange won both competitions, though mercifully neither was built. Both designs involved large-scale historicizing layouts, under the influence of roughly twelfth-century Japanese models, with lively ideological associations—and not the least dehistoricized. Tange's later postwar planning work, notably at Hiroshima, is widely known, as are his major public buildings, such as the striking and iconic Olympic Stadia at Yoyogi, Tokyo (1964). Here is not the place to rehearse Tange's career; suffice it to say that Arata Isozaki joined his studio at Tokyo University in 1953 as a fourth-year undergraduate and remained under the older architect's tutelage for a decade, eventually founding his own firm in 1963.

During these formative years, Isozaki crossed the straits of Metabolism that had opened in 1960, and about which more will be said. However, fitting together the pieces of this early formalist period and tracing the reciprocity of influence between Isozaki and Tange, Isozaki's first mature work, the Oita Prefectural Library, had more to do with the aesthetic theories of Schiller than of Schinkel. We need to bear in mind that, for all the sophistication of the architecture of the Japan Style during the 1950s as practiced by Maekawa, Sakakura, and others, the advisability of using modern Western architectural solutions in Japanese buildings had not been seriously questioned until the imposition of fascist architectural guidelines in the early years of

Showa. The postwar about-face Tange executed between the winning competition entries in the "traditional" style of the late war years and his premiated Hiroshima Atomic Memorial Museum (1949–55) is the most important indication that, in architectural terms, something momentous yet unspoken had occurred.

Not since the profound self-interrogation on matters of architectural style conducted by Sutemi Horiguchi and a few others in the early 1930s—amounting to a full generational gap—had the underlying assumptions of architectural ideology been aired. At its most acclaimed, Japanese postwar modernism endowed steel and steel-reinforced-concrete structures with the lightest of ethnic formal and material embellishments. Yet this was an emotionally freighted mix that put foreign journalists and magazine editors, as well as heads of schools and other Western architects, in aesthetic ecstasy. That was the 1950s and early 1960s, and some of the work—like Tange's Olympic Stadia—was good, and is still. But it was not what Isozaki had in mind, and he wanted to disseminate his work and have the world see his reasons.

In his long poem "The Artist" (1789), Schiller traces the development of artistic sensibility from a condition of unreflective happiness to a state in which a divided consciousness discovers a rupture between the beauty of phenomena and abstract truth and, finally, reconciles these poles through a process of acculturation and a deeper understanding of the arts. Isozaki's programmatic attempt to refound the principles of modern architecture beyond the reach of conventional Japanizing impulses, and notably the sensuous appeal of tea-garden aestheticism, if *sukiya* ramifications can be so characterized, was in some sense a latter-day equivalent. It is true that Tange had attempted to formulate the basis of a new critical self-consciousness, but always in terms that now seem either downright bizarre (witness the proposal to explicate Le Corbusier via Michelangelo), or overtly politicized—like the antithesis he designated between the archaeologically descriptive Jomon and Yayoi styles of ancient Japanese art. His intention to re-create in the Yoyogi stadia for the Tokyo Olympics a vision of the ruins of the Colisseum at Rome was perhaps closer to the mark, but succeeds to the extent this remains unintelligible to the average viewer.

Both Tange and his disciple stand in a direct line of artistic confrontation between Western prototypes and the reality of an inherited Japanese design aesthetic regarded as constrictive or even demeaning. In such designs as those for his own home, the Kurashiki Town Hall, or Yoyogi, Tange may be judged as having struck a wise balance. Yet Metabolism was proof—indeed, carried out under Tange's own sponsorship—that for a younger generation at least the issues that had plagued Japanese architects since Meiji were not yet laid to rest. Here, technology had upped the ante, and the simple metaphor—metabolism itself as an aspect of biological process—appeared to furnish a universalizing theme. After all, Kikutake, one of the prime formal and ideological contributors, had started as a medical student before turning to architecture. Yet in the Metabolist program, aspects of which Isozaki visibly retained, a factor so alien to the canons of general artistic production, whether Eastern or Western, reads as inappropriate. By equating art with sheer biological inevitability, the element of personal taste—which is the essence of *sukiya* and would be enshrined by Isozaki in the guise of *maniera*—was disposed of with the bathwater of tradition. The megastructure, that principal leitmotif of Metabolism, seems to have ridden the crest of the wave, in analogy with a feudal typology, namely the medieval Japanese castle. But that in itself was a regression to a fortresslike ideal, from which *sukiya* architecture, inspired originally by the tea cult, first provided a magnificent and truly liberating escape.

In the course of his subsequent career, the notion of *maniera* (deriving as impeccably from the sixteenth century in Europe as does that of *sukiya* in Japan) liberated Isozaki from the aesthetic and formal impasse of Metabolism. It offered him retreat from a stultifying efficiency in a nation-state where social-engineering skills are overvalued. Yet, it was not an escape into an ivory tower. To be sure, the early style of Isozaki's independent works—especially those around his hometown of Oita, in Kyushu, such as the Oita Medical Hall (1959–60), the library already mentioned, the Nakayama House (1964), and the Iwata Girls' High School of the same date—is very much a neoformalist idiom. But form in this sense was precisely the element that tradition does not provide for in Japanese architecture.

Whether or not Tange and the Metabolists had willed something of the kind in the Tokyo Plan (1960), for example, or the "future dwelling" exhibited in 1962, Isozaki's Joint-Core System or his City in the Air project of the same year, which were cruder and less poetic, nevertheless engaged with forms in a way that was uncompromising. How, or why, this should have been so will probably remain a mystery. But the issue at stake was that the Western category of "beauty" was unattainable without a commitment to form, never achieved until then in the history of Japanese architecture.

The first decisive works in this new tradition, or anti-tradition, date from the 1970s and, in terms of a simplified grandeur, come to a close most probably with the Kamioka Town Hall, completed in 1978, reverberating in the scheme for MOCA (1981–86), wherein a new level of complexity is attained. The Tsukuba Center Building was begun even earlier (1979) and, like the Los Angeles museum, is clearly of a different order, but the museum is simpler in program and massing; it seems, therefore, more closely tied to the work of the 1970s. And, in psychological terms, it represents Isozaki, having gained distance, looking back at his heroic and mature period.

Schiller's essay of 1793 entitled "Anmut und Würde," which continues to reflect the deep Kantian influence on the dramatist, now also turned theorist, dwells on the twin notions of a "state of grace" and a certain "dignity" achieved in the resolution of artistic conflict and prefigured in Shaftesbury. If one considers too much Japaneseness as a baroque perversion, as apparently Tange did at times—though, clearly, the comparison is not watertight—Schiller's poetic ideal and its relevance here are more easily grasped. It follows that neither Tange nor Isozaki have been exactly destroyers of beauty, though the "destruction" (or deconstruction) of architecture has been a slogan often on Isozaki's lips since 1975, when he published a tract aimed at the modernist canon. What Schiller does say is that beauty is the manifest achievement of freedom, that is, "freedom in appearance." Without quite destroying sensuality, its patterns are unfolded, so to speak, and its range displayed and explored. A further point, however, is that beauty in the realm of moral deliberation is a public function; thus, in order to be effective, art must be experienced publicly. With its open-ended relation between individual and collectivity, this thesis cannot but appear an extreme and difficult doctrine for the tenets of a neo-Confucianist Japanese aesthetic, even though the radical, liberating aesthetic of "tea" is in its own way a match for what Schiller has proposed. For Schiller, as for Rikyu, it is "through Beauty that man makes his way to Freedom," even if, eventually, the two approaches would have only their inspired radicality in common.

The teamaster Rikyu was, finally, unsuccessful as a political strategist, paying in 1591 with his life, at the instigation of his disciple-patron Hideyoshi. Nor were artistic perspectives opened in Japan in 1968 by the student political movement, a checkmate that Isozaki and his contemporaries have never forgotten. Thus, the most perfect of all works of art in Schiller's terms—the construction of true political freedom—was denied, or so it was perceived. And, in Isozaki's case, this provides a narrower, more poignant interpretation of his retreat into *maniera*. This dates from the late 1960s and early 1970s, the time of his works for the Fukuoka City Bank, which overlap with the official planning undertaken in collaboration with Tange's office for Expo '70 at Osaka, including Isozaki's realization of a robot-activated "cybernetic environment" for the Festival Plaza there. Though the interiors of the various bank branches and the head office were semipublic, they are introverted and lyrical—sometimes to the point of hermeticism, as emphasized by dramatic, even jarring, effects of color and lighting. By contrast, the Osaka Expo was, of course, a quasi-official manifestation of Japan, Inc., and the Festival Plaza was a supermechanized, stagelike development of Tange's earliest ideas on the uses of public space in the Greek agora. This near schizophrenic separation of roles has been stressed by Isozaki himself.

Alternatively, Isozaki's work for Tange and the nation at Expo '70 provided an essential and formative experience in a certain kind of "play"—for the robots, as has often been pointed out, were something like a giant erector set. By further analogy, Schiller, in his seminal letters "On the Aesthetic Education of Mankind" of 1794, which constitute the schema for a latter-day German classicism, offers a ready-made description of the kinetic forces Isozaki loosed, straddling the threshold of Japan's debut as a world power three decades ago. Adopting the term Fichte had employed in his Jena lectures the same year, Schiller characterized human transformational energy as the product of two drives—one toward the realization of form, the other toward that of sensation. He then postulates a third "play drive," reconciling the necessary conditions of identity and change. According to Schiller, mankind rediscovers his wholeness within a framework of aesthetic play. It is this "aesthetic mode of perception [that] makes him whole." As vital as this doctrine was in the eventual formation of European romanticism, it bears special mention here since Isozaki was the first Japanese artist to evolve a rational and conscious program putting such notions into effect. In so doing, he squared his intentions fully with the European tradition of postbaroque theory.

Isozaki, born in 1931, was old enough to have remembered something of the upheaval of World War II; and, coming from West Japan, as did Tange, he was particularly vulnerable to the trauma of the atomic destruction of Nagasaki and Hiroshima. Indeed, these were immortalized in the Electric Labyrinth, exhibited briefly by Isozaki at the 1968 Triennale in Milan. Similarly, the notion of the destruction of architecture relates, in one of its possible interpretations, to this exposure. Yet the traumas of the war in the context of the Showa era have generally been played down; without necessarily being repressed they were integrated into the cultural narrative of Japan's entry, over the space of four generations, into the modern world. In literature, the cycle of this transformation was eloquently dealt with from the beginning, while in architecture—hardly surprisingly—there had never been a Japanese Wren or Schinkel or Viollet-le-Duc, at the level of national aspirations. Instead, there were the semiprogrammatic aims of Japanese modern architecture of the 1950s and early 1960s, which, however, after 1968 seemed to lead precisely nowhere.

Though Schiller's theorizing took place in the face of the French Revolution and Schinkel's key buildings were erected in the aftermath of the Napoleonic Wars in an era of material hardship, Germany philosophy was in full flower and, for such literary and aesthetic theorists, there existed a European context. In the Japanese case, there was the immeasurable native architectural contribution, since approximately the 1850s, to the formation of European modernism. In another sense, modernism in

Japan has been muted by just this substratum of paternity. In what is the keystone of his critical and theoretical enterprise, Schiller ("On the Naive and Sentimental in Literature," 1795–96) depicts the contemporary mind as a consciousness alienated by its own experience, suspended in a state between the simplicity of its original nature and the reflective impulses contributed by culture. When Japan's unique bicultural stratification of attitudes and artifacts is added to this endemic condition of "modernism," the task of constructing a "reflective" art of self-awareness would appear to overwhelm. There is also the less obvious Oedipal strain within the Japanese relationship to modernism and, at the gates, the shock troops of postmodernism.

It is no wonder, then, that an artist and theorist as sensitive as Arata Isozaki had, by the time of his own coming of age (in Japan, something like thirty years), taken up a stand "reflective" not only in the Schillerian sense but also committed to romantic irony. In spite of Schinkel's known familiarity with the writings of Friedrich and August Wilhelm Schlegel—and, indeed, despite his romanticism—irony was visibly not a means of expression open to him. However, irony in the new romantic usage at the turn of the eighteenth century derives in part from Schiller's play-concept of art, and for Friedrich Schlegel the term is closely related to paradox, as Isozaki shows himself aware in the epigraph to this essay.

Among the elements that have bred paradox and wit in architecture, the foremost is the advent of an industrial technology, in the creation of an industrial landscape and an industrial architecture, as well as in the invention of industrially produced materials. In the history of the profession, Schinkel stands at the threshold of future developments in this connection, as does the city of Berlin. But it was not until historicism had proliferated that contrasts were held up to ridicule and exploited as ironic. So, even at the end of the nineteenth century the great Viennese architect Otto Wagner was still producing work at the very limit of the means Schinkel had devised—now enriched and empowered by a technological gadgetry but quite without concessions to irony. Adolf Loos, working a few years later also in Vienna, was a master of the biting, satirical essay on matters of building, yet even his most rhetorical built statements are without humor. Isozaki absorbed much from both these Europeans. It has been noted that Sir Edwin Lutyens was the first architect consciously to build with tongue in cheek, and he, too, is no stranger to Isozaki.

However, on the whole, it seems to me that Isozakian irony is a native product, and it may even be that "irony" in architecture was originally made possible by the *sukiya* mode. The Romans were, nonetheless, capable of working in the equivalent of Schiller's "sentimental" vein. In other words, some of their buildings do appear reflective or self-referential, as does earlier Hellenistic production. In the case of our architect, the key essay is Isozaki's early City of Ruins (1962), where fragments of a giant classical order have been recycled as megastructural design, anchored by a strip of urban freeway. The Triennale's Electric Labyrinth (1968), already referred to, takes up where this conceit leaves off, transposing the vision of urban desecration to a metropolitan scale, collaged over an image of Hiroshima. The City of Ruins has affinities with Schinkel's Royal Palace on the Acropolis, but instead of a regal and improving tableau with landscaping added, one is confronted with a patch job—and, in the Electric Labyrinth, we are terrorized.

By the 1980s, things have calmed down, so that Isozaki's realizations like the Tsukuba Center Building of 1983 or, in Tokyo, the renovation now known as the Ochanomizu Square of 1987 do, actually, in their serenity and complexity—and, above all, in their neoclassicism—resemble the late work of Schinkel, such as the Ideal Capital City or the palaces near Yalta and in Athens. Of early works by Isozaki, the last to retain traces of the mode initiated in the 1962 composition of ruins *al capriccio* or the *veduta ideata* of Hiroshima of 1968 was the Kita-kyushu City Museum of Art of 1974. This was also the first of six large public buildings after the Oita work, all of which add up to Isozaki's being the first of the post-1950s generation to complete a substantial corpus at a national scale, thus comparable with, say, the œuvre of Maekawa or Tange. The Oita sequence, from the now-to-be-destroyed medical hall of 1960 through the branch there of the Fukuoka City Bank (1967), was executed in form-faced reinforced concrete and aggressively delineated in thrusting or trabeated forms, the bank branch adding precast panels to this idiom. In 1971 the bank's head office at Hakata (Fukuoka) was the first of Isozaki's works to be faced in red Indian sandstone, a material that reappears in 1986 in The Museum of Contemporary Art, Los Angeles.

The Kita-kyushu City Museum of Art, which added an annex in 1986, is built atop a ridge and was destined to be reappropriated by the fast-growing local vegetation except for two massive caissons, square in section, aimed like a pair of binoculars at the distant landscape. Kita-kyushu was prewar Japan's prime industrial city, formerly an amalgam of townships that went on to make up a heavy industrial complex, targeted by the U.S. for destruction, in place of which, by miscalculation, Nagasaki was struck. Within the art museum much play is made with black-and-white marble paving and cascading staircases, while the twin oversize flying beams are clad in gridded cast aluminum in order to heighten a powerful sense of abstraction. The remnants of the city's industrial monuments contrast with the nonutilitarian play of the museum in repose, as pure cultural infrastructure—and artifact, a giant toy in the landscape.

Completed in the same year, 1974, is the Kita-kyushu Central Library, closer to downtown. The library, like the museum, is a longitudinal form, but here it is volute and vaulted. Taken together, library and art museum fully exploit the circle and the square, or rather the sphere and the cube, that were Isozaki's main formal repertoire during the mid-1970s. Instead of opposing the site, as the museum does, the big volumes of the library are sculpturally integrated and set off by means of a meandering staircase, also the principal landscaping element. Inside, library functions are joined by a restaurant and a museum of civic history under the same roof. In The Museum of Contemporary Art in Los Angeles, twelve years later, the architect created the same kind of milieu—half podium, half burrow—and, with its lozenges and pyramids, MOCA might be said to establish a third member, or type, in Isozaki's geometrically based sequence.

Meanwhile, also in Kyushu, near Oita but farther to the south and east, another vaulted work by Isozaki shows how different the effect of cylindrical form could be made to feel. The Fujimi Country Clubhouse (1974) was derived from Palladio's front for the Villa Poiana, itself descended from Roman architecture through Bramante, and there are additional intimations of Palladio's "Malcontenta" and Frank Lloyd Wright's Dana House at Springfield, Illinois, in various details. However, here the tunnel vault is given precedence and combined with continuous plate glazing in the apse, which forms the dining room of the clubhouse. The mood is one of repose allied with the kind of resourcefulness in adapting geometric prototypes to new functions that is the hallmark of Schinkel's mature phase and probably also the distinguishing characteristic of that architect's considerable influence, through drawings, on Frank Lloyd Wright.

In 1977 Isozaki completed a third major building in Kita-kyushu City, possibly a record in the brief history of modern Japanese townscape development. This is the West Japan General Exhibition Center, near the Kokura terminal of the Shinkansen railway and close to the port, and the largest work of the six under discussion. It consists of virtually a single expanse of support-free exhibition space protected by a roof suspended from cable-anchored masts that merge with the atmosphere of masts and cranes in the surrounding landscape. Now an annex makes use of further illusionistic and contextual devices.

Three years earlier, in 1974, Isozaki had completed the Museum of Modern Art, Gunma, in Takasaki, his first major work in the vicinity of Tokyo. Set in a parklike landscape, the museum must supply its own architectural podium. Enclosing volumetric systems have been abandoned in an obsessionist frenzy of cubical framing elements and gridded surfaces, used by Isozaki as early as the Nakayama House of 1964. Unlike the exhibition center in Kita-kyushu, the Gunma building imposes a true architectural presence, but without any rhetoric of enclosure.

The museum evokes Alvar Aalto's library of the mid-1930s at Viipuri, now a town in Russia. However, the Gunma museum is a more abstract exercise, a fact accentuated by the flat lawn. A single wing, a double windowless cube, is raised over a reflecting pool. This echoes the west wing of the original Taliesin, Wright's Wisconsin home, where the studio, canted at an angle, joins the otherwise rectilinear massing and adjoins the swimming pool. The angling of the small gallery wing at Gunma, according to the architect, preserves the building from the devastating effect of too much symmetry. Gunma is surely Isozaki's major statement about the nature and effects of architectural language—in Schiller's dichotomy, the re-reduction (of a building) to a naive, i.e., nonreferential, language. In the sculptural arrangement of giant cubical frames, which appear to make up the framing of the museum (in fact, concealing the structure), Isozaki arguably comes closer than elsewhere to the resonant new neoclassicism of Schinkel's mature phase and the neo-neoclassicism of Loos. The building fully embraces paradox at an experiential level while eschewing irony.

In the sixth and final major project of the 1970s Isozaki had the chance to fight City Hall—or redesign it—in the mining community of Kamioka, near the Japan Sea. The town offered a truly acropolitan setting, and by applying certain of the methods evolved at Gunma and crossing these with a few more ordinary classical devices, Isozaki produced both a commentary on the standard typological design of town halls and a return of architectural language from the wilder shores of abstraction, as exemplified in Gunma. The resulting Kamioka Town Hall (1978), even if profoundly schizophrenic, more than answered the program. For the sixth time in fewer than five years Isozaki produced an architectural work with the force of a public utterance, inveigling the town of Kamioka out of its vernacular darkness and isolation. As Schiller sums up in "On the Naive and Sentimental in Literature": "The poet either is nature . . . or he will seek it."

As was the theater for Schiller and Goethe, for Wright and Isozaki architecture has been an "institution of morality"; and the more so, finally, in view of the fact that these four figures of Enlightenment are fully acquainted with the sensuality of art. Yet despite this attitude of engagement, which, in Schiller's case, had he lived, would probably have precipitated a move to Berlin, where his spectacularly produced tragedies were received by an avid public, Wright felt hounded by civil society, which he came to consider in its mobocratic aspect. For Isozaki, Kamioka Town Hall was a pronouncement of the end of irony. It marks the beginning of a new Isozakian phase in which irony and paradox are appropriately, and duly, transmuted and transformed—as form.

CONCEPTUAL PROPOSAL: City in the Air

Created as a counterproposal to the planning that was under way for the skyscrapers that now dominate the Tokyo skyline in Shinjuku, this concept took issue with the prevailing notion for dividing the district into horizontally limited rectangular sections and erecting sheer vertical structures on them. Instead, the proposal suggested that the urgent need for new metropolitan architectural types could be met only by growing forms linked with each other horizontally in the air.

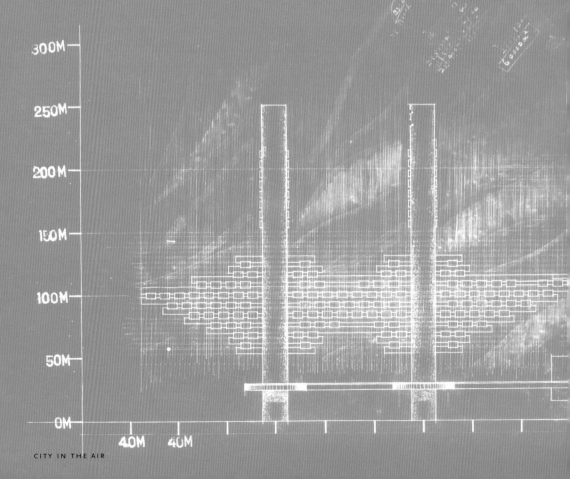

Elevation

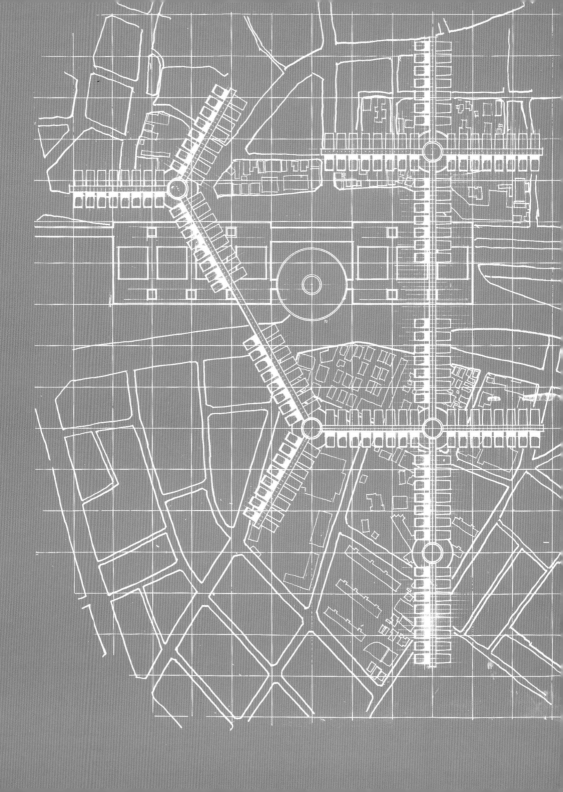

REFERENCE: Shinjuku Project (Joint-Core System)

When the skyscrapers that now crowd the skyline in the Shinjuku area of Tokyo were first proposed, a "joint core" system was offered as a counterproposal. The original development plan called for the division of the area into ordinary grids and the placement of vertically extended buildings in those delimited sites. Isozaki felt that a new type of urban architecture needed to be developed—buildings that were interconnected high above the ground that could be systematically expanded.

The infrastructure, including elevators, is contained inside cylinders called joint cores. These joint cores are linked structurally by long-span trusses, which accommodate offices spaces. The series of projects called "City in the Air" was based on this system. His intention was to expand architecture to an urban scale and to reconsider building types by introducing urban factors into architectural planning. The same system was used in "Tokyo Project 1960" prepared by the Tange studio, in the design of the central business district, which Isozaki headed.

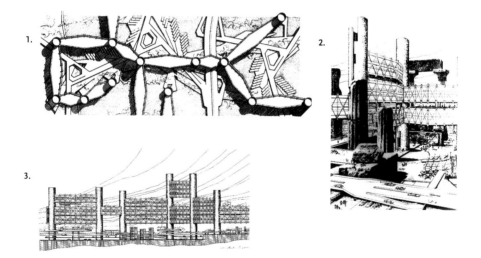

1.

2.

3.

1. Joint-core system, site plan

2. Incubation process

3. Joint-core system, main facade

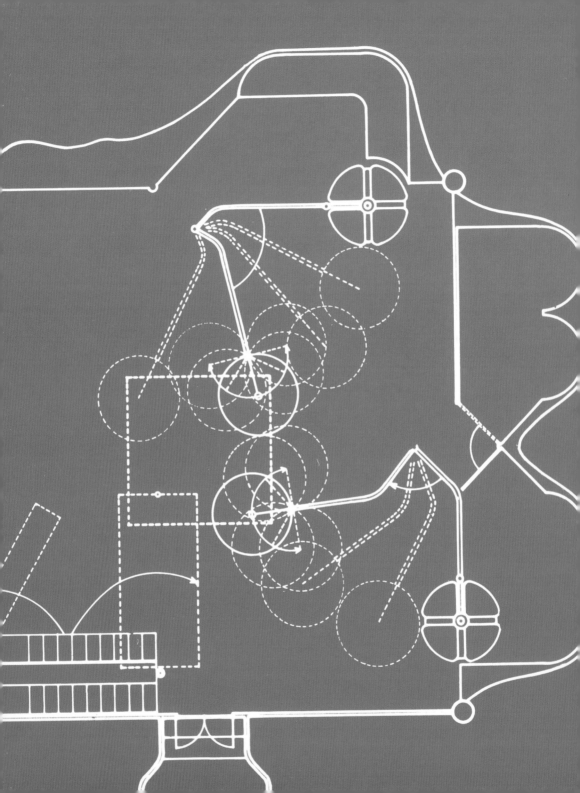

1960s: System

The sky over the archipelago was a cloudless blue on August 15, 1945, the day Japan surrendered. At that time I was a boy in my midteens and although I sensed that an era was ending, I had no idea what was beginning. All I knew was that the roaring had stopped and, for an instant, there was unmitigated calm.

Now, as I look at a photograph of a Vietnamese Buddhist priest committing self-immolation, I recall the flames of the countless foreign-made automobiles that had been overturned and set alight in front of Tokyo's Imperial Palace in 1952 on what is now called Bloody May Day. Similar flames had set ablaze the skies over Japanese cities after B29s had scattered their incendiary bombs—known as Molotov bread baskets. These had little restraining influence on me, as, in spite of the war, I continued to play in childish innocence.

Throughout my youth, until I began to study architecture, I was constantly confronted with the destruction and elimination of the physical objects that surrounded me. Japanese cities went up in flames. Forms that had been there an instant earlier vanished in the next.

The ruins that formed my childhood environment were produced by acts of sudden destruction, unlike those of Greece and Egypt, which had long been in a ruinous state. Wandering among them instilled in me an awareness of the phenomenon of obliteration, rather than a sense of the transience of things.

On the day in 1960 when the Japanese-American Security Treaty was ratified, I was a member of a protest demonstration in front of the Prime Minister's official residence. An abandoned armored car had been parked sideways across a narrow sloping street beside the residence, and a group that seemed to be right-wing had occupied it. They probably thought this side street, which was blocked, would be an excellent place to trap and thrash any of the protesting students and citizens milling around the Diet building. I was part of a barricade intended to isolate the armored car. As it grew late and we all began to feel tired, both groups mingled and joked with each other until it was impossible to tell friend from foe.

For about a week I had patrolled the Diet building and by the time the ratification took place, late at night, I was very weary. In previous demonstrations, I had been obsessed with the fantasy of seeing the Diet building, which looks like a preposterously large gravestone, set alight like the buildings that I had seen during the war. Although a female student who tried to crash into the Diet was killed, there was no fire. The tension in our group began to crumble that night. I happened to catch a glimpse of the eyes of a man, who all night, virtually without moving, had stood in a position of leadership on top of the armored car, waiting for a signal. He and his group must have experienced a despair more dreadful than ours.

After the struggle over the treaty was finished, the two things that remained in my memory in connection with it were the Diet building, which did not go up in flames after all, and the eyes of the man who, then, at any rate, was my enemy.

At about this time a group of my artiest friends began behaving in eccentric ways on busy street corners. Calling themselves the Neo-Dadaist Organizers, they rashly opposed everything connected with existing institutions, organizations, and systems. I sympathized with their belief that only destructive behavior can be called art and sometimes participated in their activities. At one point, Shusaku Arakawa, a member of the group, and I proposed planning a house that would be impossible to live in—of course the plan was never realized.

In 1960, the Metabolist Group was formed and began designing cities of the future. The members of the group were friends, all about my age. Whereas they were all independent architects attempting to establish their own methodologies, I was still employed in the offices of Kenzo Tange and URTEC, where I was in charge of the "Tokyo Plan," a scheme for a futuristic city stretching its backbone over the waters of Tokyo Bay. The spare time I had after work was spent engaged in political demonstrations and the antiproductive debauchery of artists' groups, leaving me very little freedom for planning on my own.

The thinking behind Japanese architecture in the 1950s had been to attempt to unify traditional Japanese wooden structures with Modernist architectural space, in which interior and exterior could interpenetrate. It could be termed a Japanese version of the New Empiricism and New Brutalism popular in Europe at the time. The Metabolists proposed bold technical innovations and, by means of their proposals for cities of the future, attempted to break the current architectural thinking. In the 1960s Japan experienced miraculous economic growth, consequently cities were rebuilt and expanded. Metabolism's ideas and methods accurately reflected prevailing circumstances, making it the leading architectural ideology of the time.

Metabolist architecture celebrated an industrial society. These architects believed that architecture was a durable consumer item. Consequently, their use of exterior capsules, units, and panels was not necessarily a solution founded in theory but lauded the industrial society by displaying mass-produced elements and indicating the ways in which they could be replaced and altered.

I was dissatisfied with politics, art, and my own field of architecture in 1960, but unable to break through with a methodology of my own, I became frustrated and day after day spent my energy on physical participation in radical activities.

At about that time, I was given a chance to publish a project entitled "Incubation Process" in an art magazine. In this context I abandoned all the technical considerations with which, as an architect and planner, I had been compelled to deal, and concentrated solely on the materialization of a concept that was then in the process of genesis.

The result was a simple photomontage that was extremely illogical and therefore neither architecture, poetry, urban planning, philosophy, a picture, a comic, nor a diagram. This photomontage liberated me from psychological suppression. By cutting ties with the architect's methods, the rational support of which is technology, I felt that I was once again able to strive to be an architect. Forced into a corner and almost desperate, I had discovered a breakthrough.

Later, this photograph was frequently cited as a representative Metabolist work. But while I was certainly thinking in Metabolist terms in this montage, as I dealt with the flux of generation and the destruction of the city, I was never a member of the Metabolist group. Indeed, I always tried to make a clear distinction between myself and their technological orientation, their somewhat naive pragmatism which allowed them to believe that a social revolution could be achieved by means of new technology.

My next task was to define the image of the kind of architect I wanted to be. The following passage, from some of my notes written in about 1960, has a bearing on this image:

> In my opinion, the minimum requirement of an architect is a concept that germinates within himself. Though it may correspond organically to reason, design, and all the phenomena of actuality and nonactuality, this concept must exist without connection with any of these things. The existence of the concept can be proven only when the concept itself can be conveyed to others. It probably becomes certain and unshakable in accordance with the nature of the medium through which it is conveyed; I want to discover the medium that will make possible its most accurate transmission. . . . In the search, architectural design is my professional means.

To discover the concept, I sought ideas for the interpretation of space, time, and matter (architecture and cities), all three solely as metaphors. My equations for them are space = darkness; time = termination (eschatology); and matter, or architecture and cities = ruin and ashes. I have written essays on all three topics: "Space of Darkness," "Process Planning," and "Invisible City." Darkness, termination, and ruin are incapable of being given form; they are diametrically opposed to such socially recognized concepts as transparency, progress, and construction, and have an aura of the unfortunate about them. Although I considered a paradoxical stance using these concepts as an effective means of countering architecture as it existed at the time, when technology reigned supreme, no one in the Japanese architectural world took me seriously.

Oddly enough, these metaphorical images relate to my memory of that instance of total tranquility, when everything seemed to have stopped, that I experienced on the day of the Japanese surrender. The houses and buildings that we had considered mainstays of our way of life, the established belief of the national state with the Emperor at its head, and the social system that controlled even the smallest daily activities, had been destroyed and had vanished, leaving behind only the void of the blue sky overhead.

Infinite darkness lies behind the blue sky. The stopping of time is a termination like the eschatological interpretation of the end of the world. The burned-out cities that I saw before me were ruins. Perhaps subconsciously I am attempting to return to that remembered instant that changed history and to conceptualize that moment in the form of architecture.

1965 MEDIA, ILLUSION, VOID: INVISIBLE CITY

It is perfectly acceptable to consider cities as a flux of generation and destruction but, in doing so, the nature of time must be examined. Having learned the ideas of mobility and change from Team X, the Metabolist architects attempted to think of architecture and cities in terms of the Buddhist idea of transmigration. They made no general observations, instead they proposed the concrete mechanism of architectural composition: a more or less permanent framework with changeable elements plugged into it and a smooth order governing the relations between the two. As the name of the movement reveals, they took the metabolism of organic creatures as the model of the kind of change they posited. Without delving into the philosophy of time, they were more concerned with the foreseen harmony of alteration systematically taking place within the flow of the time in which transmigration takes place.

I was in agreement with most of what they said but could not see eye to eye on one cardinal point: drawing a direct analogy between organic metabolism and architectural composition. For rather than being systematic, change is dramatic and destructive, lying outside the bonds of human control. It is the result of complicated accumulations of overlapping, unforeseeable coincidences. Method and logic originate on the basis of a toleration of the natural course of change.

Since change is half-destructive and half-constructive, it should be permissible for architecture to create the exact appearance of ruins.

When Tokyo was rebuilt after World War II, it accommodated examples of the weird generation of accumulated coincidences. The cheap room I rented as a college student was located in one of these disorderly places. The wooden building, a capricious conglomeration of repeated additions located on a gently sloping bank, was devoid of the systematic placement, lucidity, and order that are generally recognized as the characteristics of traditional Japanese residential architecture. To reach my room, which was in the innermost part of the building, one walked up two or three steps and down a diagonal corridor, then up a flight of stairs that turned twice along the way, then down a corridor leading to the left and up still another flight of steps. The side of the bank was covered with an irregular mass consisting of a small part of the original building plus a number of additions necessitated over the years by dismantling and alterations of function and repairs.

In later years I tried referring to it as a topological labyrinth, but actually the neighborhood was a slum. Before the war it was a rundown region for poor laborers, now it was a sunless ravine and bank on which my boardinghouse was located. Small houses crowded in on each other, and no doubt the cats that wandered from roof to roof had a better idea of the overall space than the human inhabitants.

My boardinghouse was not level and plumb: the books that I arranged along one wall were so heavy that my room gradually tilted in that direction. From time to time the landlord would prop it up. My first priority was to move, but before I did I became interested in the entire region and its complicated spaces: the disjointed spatial connections; the spontaneous happenings; the capricious appearance and disappearance of spaces; the conjunctions of multifarious and diverse functions; the many layered spaces; the corridors that twisted like a Möbius strip; doors that produced both awful noises and beautiful voices; and people living together with rats, ticks, goldfish, and grasshoppers.

Ruins clearly reveal themselves in the process of construction and alteration. In the war many Japanese cities lost all their old forms, but they were rapidly filled with groups of buildings that, from the very outset, looked like ruins with no visual order. Steel and concrete mixed with advertisements; neon lights and telegraph poles came into and passed out of existence easily. Cities lost their monumentality behind an aggregation of flickering, lightweight, and superficial elements. They began to convey their meanings to us through semiotic codes rather than actual solid forms. The development of various kinds of new media intensified this trend.

The city is undeniably in a state of flux. Invisible, it is virtually simulated by the codes that fill it. In my "Invisible City," which alludes to ruins, I foresaw a city filled with unreal codes where the interpretation of the classical structure of cognition is meaningless. I now believe that design and city planning will become impossible using methods that involve only the manipulation of physical actualities. Since coming to this conclusion, although I regard cities as fit objects for consideration, I have ceased to think that they can be designed and hence no longer undertake work of that kind.

In thinking about architecture, more than the city, time reveals itself in naked form. Designing a building, of course, means making visible something that has never before existed. The time involved in composing a piece of architecture is absolute and essentially different from time as expressed in the change and metamorphosis of the Metabolist architects. In "Process Planning," I interpret time in architecture from a completely different viewpoint. The idea of "growing architecture," which was popular when I wrote the article, is the reverse of the process that produces ruins.

In the normal process of creating architecture, at the final minute it is necessary to freeze all alteration. In the search for that moment of freedom, I made use of the ancient Judaic eschatological principle that the world must someday come to an end. Imagining the ultimate end is a dynamic viewpoint, clarifying the direction in which present conditions flow. On the drawing board, the piece of architecture is allowed to grow and change until it reaches its ultimate point in time, its termination, then it is cut off at the juncture called the present. It is then fixed and leaves the architect's hands. It may change thereafter, but it is meaningless to try, as the Metabolists did, to foresee its future alterations. It is not for the architect to speak of its future.

In this connection, the time that exists in the architect's concept emerges. This is different from absolute time, which flows unbroken from the past to the future.

In explaining the moment of enlightenment, the great Buddhist priest Dōgen (1200–1253), the first person to give Zen teachings a firm systematic foundation in Japan, wrote of flying toward a given instant. However, the same notion of time has existed in the Orient since the distant past. For instance, in the *Abhidharma-kosha-shastra,* the fifteenth-century Buddhist priest and scholar Vasubandhu clearly defines time as a single moment. Everything before the emergence of a dharma (entity) is the past and everything after its disappearance is the future. The moment before the eyes is the present. In this version, time is included within the entity.

In my architectural method I combine the dynamism of the Judaic idea of termination and the Buddhist concept of time as reduced to the instant. The final section of "Process Planning" sets forth the way in which architecture that has grown in reverse from the terminal minute is frozen in an instant. In other words, the building ceases to progress toward growth and instead begins moving in the direction of ruin. For this reason, my doctrine lacks the optimism derived from the future of eschatological thought and is closer to the Buddhist doctrine of the impermanence of all things.

Many of the ideas that went into the formulation of this viewpoint were developed during work on a joint research project that resulted in a volume called *Niho no toshi kūkan* (Japanese Urban Space). This study revealed that many of the characteristics of Japanese cities cannot be adequately explained on the basis of Western urban concepts. Our study was a method of analyzing those elements.

The traditional Japanese city consisted of buildings made largely of wood, paper, and straw, which could easily be turned to ashes, and did not readily reveal itself to the eye. It was governed by a vague awareness of the mood of a busy neighborhood (*kaiwai*). I have come to think that the old-fashioned neighborhood feeling is becoming a characteristic of the modern Japanese city too.

Work on this project resulted in "Invisible City" and led to the development of the idea of "Darkness" as an architectural prototype.

Counterpoising invisibility and darkness with highly visible and substantial cities and architecture made my methodology more conceptual and metaphorical. Architectural design is the process of giving concrete form to intangible concepts. In this process it is first necessary to pick out all the things that denote architectural elements; then it is necessary to create a mechanism that will give new meaning to these now neutralized elements. This is the starting point of my architecture.

ARATA ISOZAKI

OITA PREFECTURAL LIBRARY

Oita, Japan, 1962–66

Overall view from the northeast

The site for this public library is very close to the Oita Medical Hall, completed six years earlier. The medical hall was Isozaki's first building of a public nature, designed independently while he was still working with Kenzo Tange. But the library was the first official public commission, and it was substantial enough to enable him to set up his own design firm, Arata Isozaki Atelier.

Still showing the influence of Metabolism, this design was initially conceived as "growing architecture," and the preliminary proposal was published together with an essay exploring the notion of "process planning." The elements were classified by program into several types with different dimensions, and the basic structural system was designed to allow for extensions of floor area according to these dimensions. The interconnecting sections between parts became the primary image for the design, in which the appearance of the whole was secondary to growth patterns developed through these nodes.

The initial proposal had principal component structures formed into prefabricated units, which were stacked on top of each other. However, financial constraints forced the substitution of the original finish with cast-in-place concrete. At the time, this was the most readily available material in Japan to provide a good-quality finish at a reasonable cost. The design of the interiors also had to be considerably simplified.

The reinforced-concrete building frame is divided into a core section, delimited by paired walls, and subsidiary units composed around protuberant, box-shaped beams containing both air-conditioning ducts and circulation spaces. What is seen from the exterior is the repetition of room units enclosed in the wall pairs and distributed around the exposed box beams. Extending out from the central zone—the core of the functional system—are the units containing reading rooms, stacks, and service areas, as well as administration offices and other ancillary facilities. These extensions are supported by box frames with thicker sides.

The original inspiration for the design was an analogy with the human body's skeletal system (concrete skeleton), circulatory system (ducts), and musculature (interior spatial composition)—with obvious affinities to the interconnected trunk, branches, and leaves underlying the Joint-Core System. Although traces of these origins remain in the structure as built, exposed concrete is the overwhelming force in the finished expression.

Entrance hall

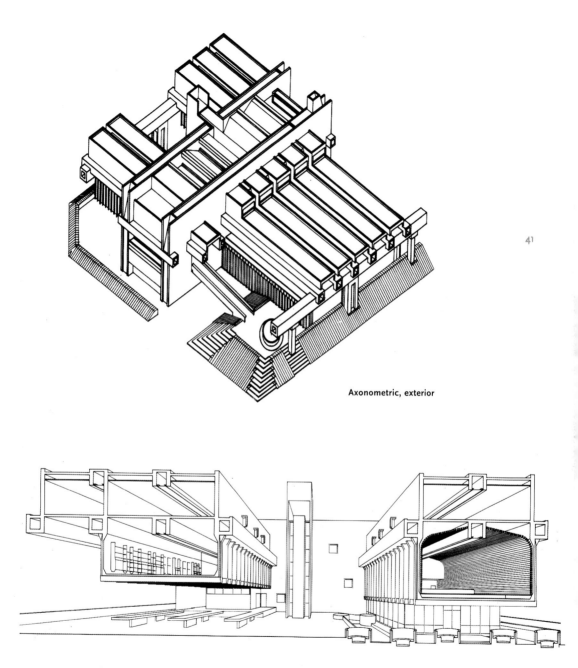

Axonometric, exterior

Sectional perspective, south wing

Bridge over browsing hall

View of browsing hall

FUKUOKA CITY BANK HEAD OFFICE AND ADDITION

Fukuoka, Japan, 1963–71 (head office) and 1978–83 (addition)

Isozaki Atelier, which had designed several branches of the Fukuoka City Bank (formerly the Fukuoka Mutual Bank), was asked to create their new headquarters on a site across from Hakata Station in Fukuoka, Kyushu. Design was initiated in 1968, and construction was completed in 1971. Ten years after the commission for the head office, new designs were required for an addition on a neighboring site.

The Oita Prefectural Library is the prime example of the architectural and structural techniques developed by Isozaki in the 1960s. There the central zone, the core of the architectural system, is bounded by paired walls, and other functional elements are projected out from the core. This design concept is developed on a much larger scale for the Fukuoka City Bank Head Office. During the design process the specifications for floor space and the number of rooms were changed several times, and provisions had to be made for expected fluctuations in floor-space requirements that would continue after the building was finished. The clients also needed a scheme that was open to expansion, as they were planning for extensions every ten years or so. The first of these was designed in 1978.

The overall structure is defined by two large walls running parallel along the full length of the site (260 feet) and rising to 160 feet, the maximum height permitted due to air traffic from the nearby airport. To house the required spaces at high levels, the core section has projections front and back in which rooms are arranged in units. The first floor of the forward section contains the banking hall, and at the back is the parking garage; on the next level are administrative offices, with executive offices on top. Just as in the Oita Prefectural Library, the total image is established by the subordination of the variously shaped elements to the imposing central core with its great walls.

The high-rise section is faced in red Indian sandstone, whose color and surface texture are enhanced by the strong light characteristic of this area in the south of Japan. Sandstone was used again for MOCA, also in a location with strong sunlight (southern California), and in that regard the bank was an important precedent in the design of the art museum.

Sepia-colored Cor-ten steel was selected for the protruding units in the lower structure to match the red sandstone, while red granite was used for the surfaces of the huge beams receiving their sections. Wide cylinders containing rooms and stairways stand like circular columns on the exterior of the banking hall, establishing the bank's monumental presence across from the station plaza.

Exterior detail

Exterior wall, faced in red Indian sandstone

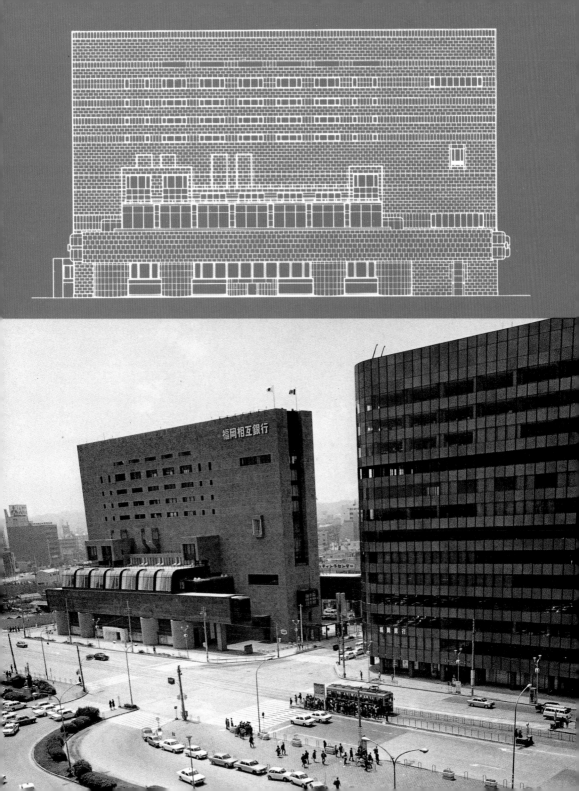

Interior view

Reception room

Interior view

N HOUSE

Oita, Japan, 1964

Located in the downtown area of a city that was on the verge of high-rise development, this project called for a clinic and a residence in separate buildings (an urban residence type called a *machiya* in Japanese) that were protected from outside views. The image underlying the design was inspired by the handling of light and atmosphere in Vermeer's paintings. The quartered streetfront windows of old Dutch townhouses are referred to here in the four clerestory windows grouped in the center of the roof, but they are transformed by the need to have daylight entering at an angle from above.

Although the desire was to design a three-dimensional composition of pure Platonic forms, it did not seem feasible because the method of lighting dictated a specific division of rooms and structures. This problem was resolved only by departing from modern architecture's credo that spatial division should conform to function. The solution was two completely unrelated internal systems—the primary structure (determined by the lighting method), and the layout for furniture, storage spaces, and domestic artifacts—which were designed separately and simply put together. Discontinuities and skewed elements appear throughout, perhaps most distinctly in the relationship between the clerestories and the placement of equipment, and pointing out these disjunctions is one of the main design themes.

Before the big buildings went up, the N House stood on its own in serene isolation; it was not long, however, before it was completely surrounded. But this hermetic microcosm was designed to be insulated from the outside world, to have its autonomy secured as land, space, and sky were closed off all around. The design was severely criticized by many observers at the time because it so completely cut off its surrondings; but it was a particular response to a very special program and was not intended as a general solution.

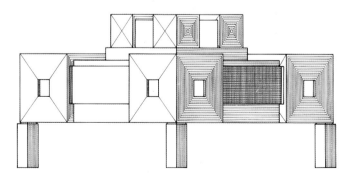

Elevation

Night view

This project is a model of a technological house designed to be maximally responsive, allowing occupants to change layouts at will based on simple domestic devices like Japanese *shoji* screens. The hinge is the key to this solution.

1.

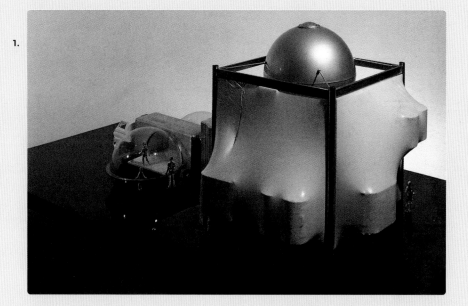

2.

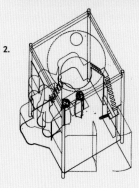

1. Model, exterior view   **2.** Axonometric

3.

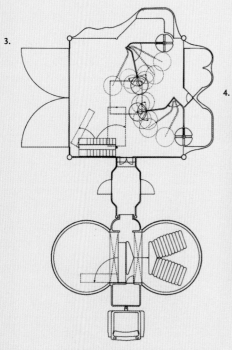

4.

5.

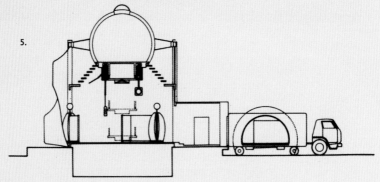

3. Floor plan   **4.** Model, exterior view   **5.** Section

Living room

Living room

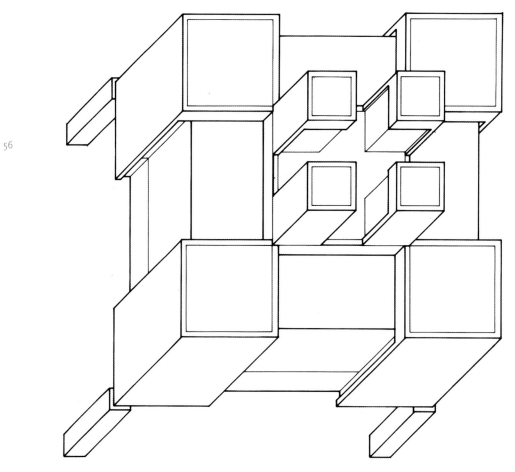

Axonometric

Of the two separate structures here—a clinic and a house—the design for the latter was derived from an earlier project, the Responsive House, whose cross section is now extruded in one direction. The principal daytime domestic space—the living and dining area—is situated on the first floor. The suspended spherical bedroom of the Responsive House is transformed here into a central vaulted structure containing a study and a bedroom.

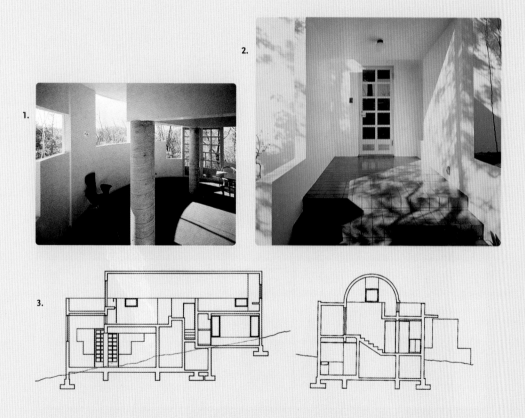

1. Living room   **2.** Entrance   **3.** Sections

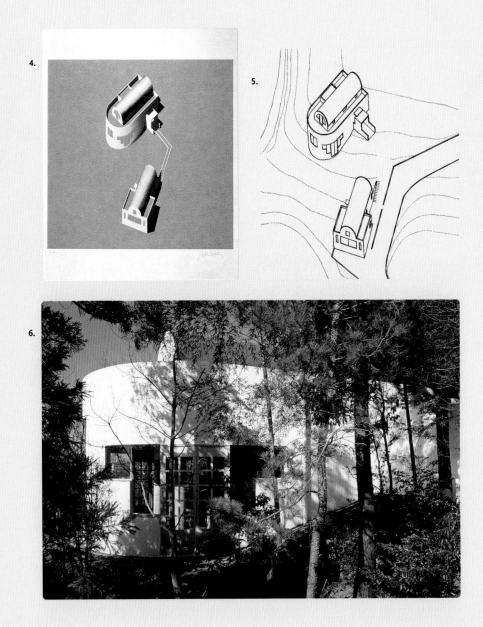

4. Axonometric, silk-screen

5. Axonometric

6. The house in its setting, exterior view

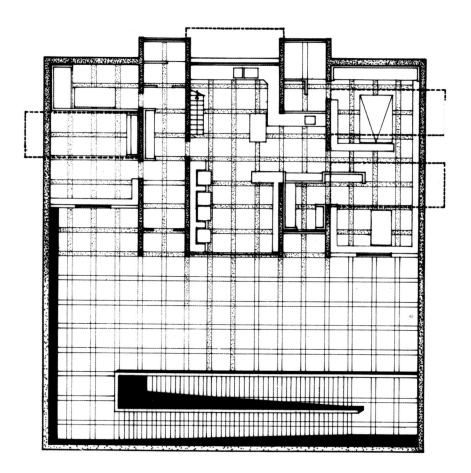

Second-floor plan, first scheme

REFERENCE: Aoki House

Beyond the requirements of site and program, the shape and character of this small urban residence were determined by severe restrictions on materials and an extreme simplification of the skeleton. Structurally it is made up of four void slab portal units, the ends left open, stacked on top of each other. With this slab system, stairways can be located only on the outside. At the top of the structure is a vaulted roof, but here it is larger than in previous residences (eighteen instead of twelve feet in diameter), and it is pierced on one side by a much smaller one.

1.

2.
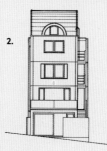

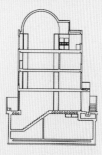

3.

1. Axonometric, silk-screen

2. (L) South elevation
(R) Section

3. Top vault window

REFERENCE: Björnson Studio

This studio and residence faces a narrow street not far from the oceanfront road along Los Angeles's Venice Beach, known for its rollerskaters. It was originally designed as a guest house for artists, and the program called for a studio and basic living quarters that would permit a visitor to stay and work for an extended period of time.

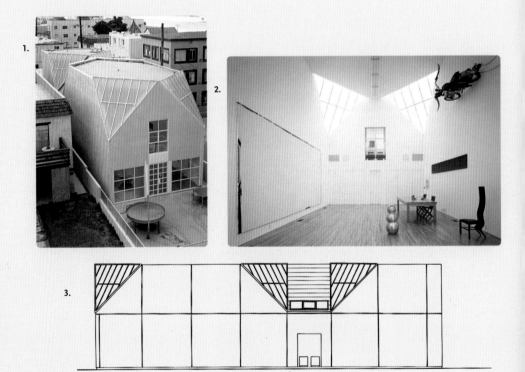

1. View of the terrace, with the ocean in the distance

2. The gallery space

3. Elevation

Ceiling of living room

CONCEPTUAL PROPOSAL: Festival Plaza, Expo '70

Osaka

Expo '70 was conceived as an international event to celebrate Japan's rapid economic growth during the 1960s. Isozaki participated in drawing up the master plan, proposing the concept for the central facility of the exhibition spaces, the Festival Plaza. The intention here was to orchestrate theatrical space that could bring together a large number of performers and visitors, using a variety of new technologies. The variable, computerized components—a roof that could be opened to the sky; robots moving on the ground; sound, lighting, and other equipment hanging from above; movable seating—would make for a truly "cybernetic environment."

Festival Plaza

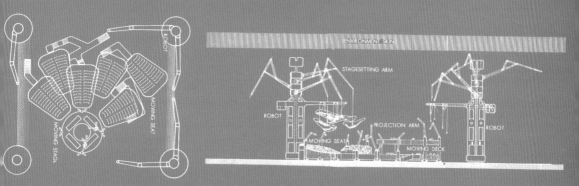

A set of mechanical apparatuses

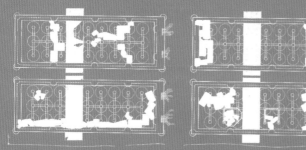

A set of mechanical apparatuses

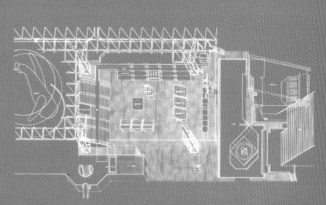

Axonometric, Festival Plaza

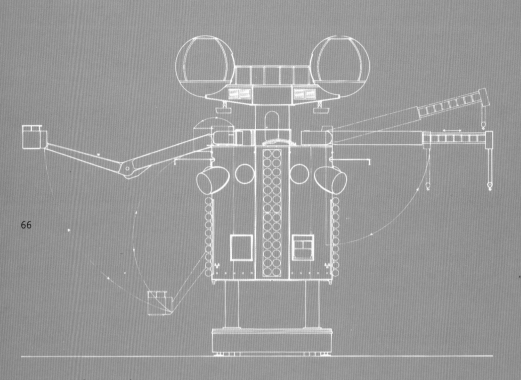

Performance robot

Performance robot

Combining the concept of computer-supported urban space with that of the "festival plaza" leads to something like a cabled city, animated by information exchanged through coaxial lines. Today data transmission is restricted to the one-way systems of current TV and radio, but coaxial cables can easily handle the transmission of large volumes of data in both directions. With this network in place, a supercomputer for information exchange, processing, and storage could function as the "brains" of the city. Although cities may now be capable of handling the distribution of information, the constant flow of massive quantities of visual and tactile information can be processed only with advanced technology.

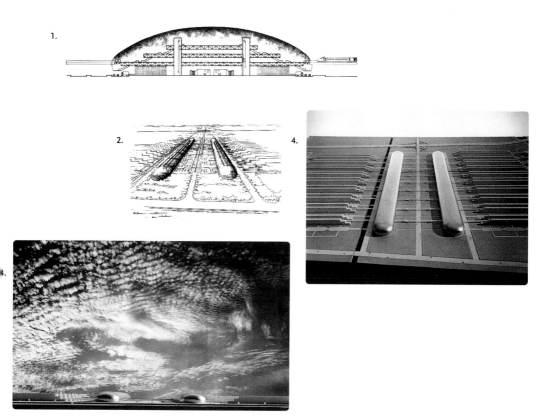

1. Section   **2.** Perspective   **3.** Elevation view of the model   **4.** Perspective view of the model

REFERENCE: The Palladium Club

The Academy of Music, a New York opera house building in 1926, became the Palladium, a popular rock concert hall in the 1970s. However, during the 1960s and '70s, the area surrounding this theater had rapidly degenerated, which affected this theater as well. With this project, it was possible to carry out a thorough renewal of the interior architecture while maintaining its external appearance. Looking at the structure from the outside, one would never guess the extent of the transformation achieved within.

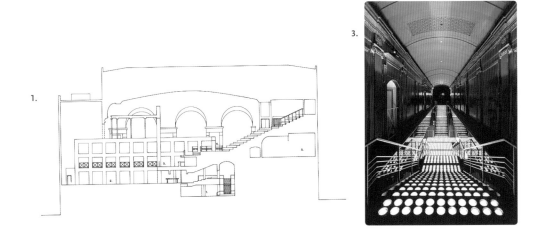

1. Section

2. Nested boxes: belvedere to the baroque movements on the dance floor

3. Main stairs

FESTIVAL PLAZA, EXPO '70

4.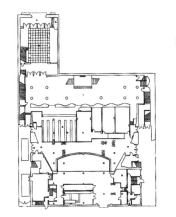

5.

6.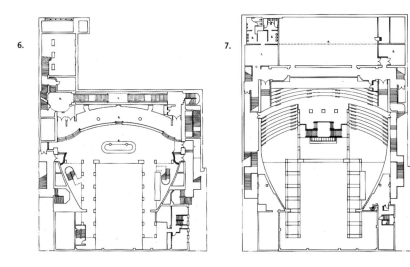

7.

4. Ground-floor plan   **5.** The dance floor   **6.** Main dance-floor plan   **7.** Michael Todo room-level floor plan

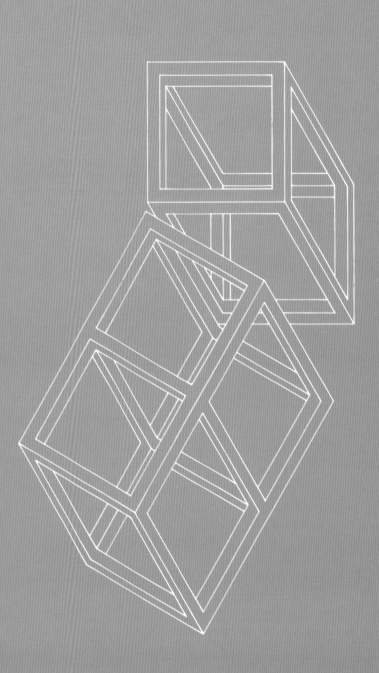

1970s: Metaphor

REDUCTION TO THE BLANK: METHOD, MANNER

In some respects, 1968 may be compared with 1527, when papal Rome was sacked, occupied, and pillaged by the Spanish. Although the Spanish occupation was only temporary and papal authority was restored with the passage of time, this incident destroyed Rome's character as a cultural center and gave birth to the possibility of Mannerism.

In 1968, the Chinese Cultural Revolution ignited sparks all over the world that fired young people to acts of demonstration. Schools, offices, and galleries were occupied, and liberated zones were set up in many great cities. Although strategic areas were targeted, most of these uprisings were spontaneous attempts to overthrow the Establishment and transcend the boundaries between right and left, or conservative and revolutionary.

I was pleased to observe this explosion of anarchic energy since I viewed it as agreeing with my own program for the overthrow of architectural Modernism. Some years earlier, I had designed the Oita Prefectural Library, which was made with unfinished concrete—"*bêton brut.*" This building was the Japanese realization of the New Brutalism, and I was signifying my graduation from all the things I had learned from Modernism up to that point. The next task was the dissolution of Modernism.

Ridding myself of a Modernism that pervaded my whole being was difficult. It was a tautological paradox to attempt to employ Modernist vocabulary, the only vocabulary I could use, in dismembering Modernism. Such was my dilemma in 1968.

In May of that same year, I was put in charge of a corner at the fourteenth Milan Triennale. My project, which was called "Electric Labyrinth," used light, projections, sound, and music to involve the visitor in a technologically created environment. In the display, ghost-figures from the Edo period of Japanese history (1600–1867) overlapped with the ruins of Hiroshima and the destruction of the city of the future in what amounted to a criticism of modern urban planning for doing no more than painting rosy, utopian pictures. From the day of the opening ceremonies, however, my space was occupied by someone else. In the hall were a few other works reflecting ideas similar to my own, but no matter what the ideas, everything had to fit into the established Triennale pattern. This may be why my place was taken from me. From the outset, this exhibition was intended to celebrate and circulate products of the industrial society. It is self-contradictory to attempt to criticize modern design through Modernism. I repeatedly asked myself whether the only way to shake the system was to resort to violent contestation.

At the same time, I found myself in a very difficult situation in connection with the World Exposition held in Osaka in 1970 (Expo '70). As a representative of Kenzo Tange, the general producer, I was personally responsible for designing the equipment for Festival Plaza—the central facility of the entire exposition. In addition, I was technical producer for the opening-day ceremonies. A national event like a world exposition is naturally an important target for debate, and I was criticized for taking part in it. While emotionally sympathetic to my critics, whose views I understood, I nevertheless had a professional architect's responsibility to complete work that had long been contracted.

At one time, brilliantly colored spaces began to fade, the shadows began to disappear from objects with definite outlines, and the sense of their existence began to grow vague. I cannot say precisely when I started to see things in this way, although I suspect it was probably while making preparations for Expo '70, which always reminded me of a space in which a box of toys had been overturned.

At the time, I acted like the headmaster in those preparations: making proposals, drawing-up working plans, taking part in the activities of site-control groups, and advocating color-scheme diversity. Then, when everything was as I wished, it was impossible for me to cry out that everything was wrong—but it was wrong. I could tell that something invisible and indefinite was missing behind the displays, the organization, the shows, the crowds, and the information media. I witnessed the process from which the deficiency came.

I was overcome with tremendous fatigue. When this happened, images that had formerly presented themselves to me in bright colors faded like overexposed photographs, leaving nothing but tones of sepia and white. Fatigue was not the whole problem. I was completely, physically rundown. I collapsed one morning and had to leave the Expo grounds in a wheelchair that was loaded on a Boeing 727 with a forklift. It happened on the very day when the Emperor and the Crown Prince visited the Expo grounds and when the robots I had designed danced to the *Kima ga yo* (the Japanese national anthem) as flower petals rained down from the great roof covering the Festival Plaza.

For months I lay idle in bed, once again the victim of a psychosomatic crisis that visits me at intervals of about a decade. This was the gravest seizure I had yet experienced. The first time I had been stricken, ten years earlier, fatigue had been the cause. I now concluded I had to leave the Kenzo Tange office and set up on my own. Confronting hospital gloom, I resolved then to make darkness and ruin the basis of my theories of space and time.

I had found myself in the embarrassing position of being a critic of Modernism who was taking a professional part in Expo '70, a national event in which the Modernist vocabulary was the only one permitted. This predicament created great nervous tension and ruined me physically. Under these circumstances, colors faded for me and I began to see only blanks. Substances lost mass and became only shadows. I felt as if twilight, known as the devil's hour, had settled on the whole world. I resolved that when I designed buildings from that time forward I would pursue the blank as far as possible, to return physical objects to a colorless state, and to formulate the way I did this into a methodology.

Making multidimensional spaces from concrete objects necessitates basic lines and compositional units to serve as minimal clues. Though they were my ultimate concepts, from the standpoint of physical architecture, blankness and twilight can be nothing but metaphors achieved by means of neutralized geometry and meticulously controlled conditions of light-beam distribution. The device that I ultimately hit on was the use of a grid composed of homogenous, limitless, square compartments to cover exterior surfaces. My entire visible world was to be covered with this grid of equal squares.

The trap inherent in this situation is the impossibility of covering surfaces with anything other than minimal units. This is where geometrical figures must come into play.

It is essential to seek forms that have been reduced to their minimum, since they are the only ones that can be used in actualizing blanks. The square is abstracted from the equally divided grid, and the circle, which encompasses unit surface with the minimum outline, comes to mind. Applied multidimensionally in architecture, the square and circle generate the cube, the cylinder, the sphere, and the regular tetrahedron; composed of right angles and enclosing a minimum volume with equal sides. From ancient times, these naturally evolved, basic forms have been called the Platonic solids.

At the time of my second crisis, I had arrived at the point where I was determined to reorganize and reduce all my architecture to the forms of the Platonic solids. During this reorganization, the tide of protest that heralded a season of political reform suddenly ebbed. However, Modernist architecture had clearly completed its union with the authorities in control.

In 1527, the sack of Rome by the Spanish destroyed Rome's importance as a cultural center. In my view, in 1968, the collapse of both seamy-side functionalism and the Modernist concept of progress toward utopia through the leadership of the avant-garde served as a boundary. Thereafter, Modernism in architecture lost its social effectiveness.

Reduction to the blank and attachment to the Platonic solids constituted my criticism of Modernist architecture. A tendency toward formalism was my political choice for the 1970s, and I organized it into the doctrine that I describe as *maniera*.

ARATA ISOZAKI

THE MUSEUM OF MODERN ART, GUNMA

Takasaki, Gunma, Japan, 1971–74

The first of Isozaki's many commissions for modern and contemporary art museums was received from Gunma Prefecture in 1971. After the cultural revolutions of 1968 and the exhausting work on the national project Expo '70, Isozaki felt that there was no other way to proceed in design and in the analysis of architectural programs than to trace every form, every concept, back to its origins. Only pristine, essential structures seemed to offer hope of finding new points of departure. The Museum of Modern Art, Gunma, was the first of Isozaki's designs to be executed in this spirit.

The cube—the equilateral volumetric unit—was clearly the form to begin with for the new approach. The design problem then became developing the spatial distribution from arrangements of and continuities between this basic shape as applied to the requirements of the program. The cubic framework was also taken up as a metaphor for the art museum of today, where the gallery has become a kind of port into and out of which artworks move. No mere structural device, the cube here represents the idea of the art gallery as void.

The design is based on the interaction of two architectural systems: the skeletal parti of forty-foot cubes (the basic structure) and the exhibition spaces, stairways, administrative offices, lighting, and so on (the supplemental structure). The series of cubes, laid out on an expansive lawn in a parklike setting, takes the form of one large rectangular block, which houses the main exhibition space, and two shorter, projecting wings. The first of these is perpendicular to the central block and contains the entrance hall. The second, angled off the building's primary axis, holds a gallery for traditional Japanese art. This wing is elevated above a square reflecting pool, with an open terrace at the first-floor level.

The entire south side of the building is clad in four-foot-square panels of aluminum or glass, creating a gleaming, gridded facade. Although the rear (north) elevation was also meant to be covered in aluminum, it was left in exposed concrete due to financial constraints.

Principles of framing, grids, flush surfaces, and other aspects of this design were later applied to the new master plan for the Brooklyn Museum.

Perspective, conceptual structure

The west cube beside the central stair and entry spine serves as a frame around the entrance hall.

Overall view from the southwest

Entrance hall, view looking southwest

View looking west, with the low gallery and tiled terrace

View of the Temporary Exhibition Gallery

In the design of this building—the headquarters of the Shuko-sha company, which specializes in printing and advertising—the basic structure is related to the ancillary structure, but in a different way from the museum at Gunma. Here, the lower level of a two-level, three-dimensional frame is filled with walls and punched windows; the upper level, with gridded glass that clearly reveals the frame. An exhibition room and a multipurpose hall are on the first and second floors, offices on the third and fourth floors, and the owner's office and conference room on the top floor. The 9.6-meter grid imposes a large framework but does not determine the ceiling heights from floor to floor. Adjusting these heights produced rooms with different shapes and sizes.

1.

2.

3.

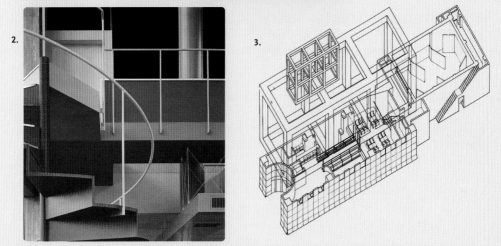

1. Fifth-floor interior   **2.** Handrail of stairs   **3.** Axonometric

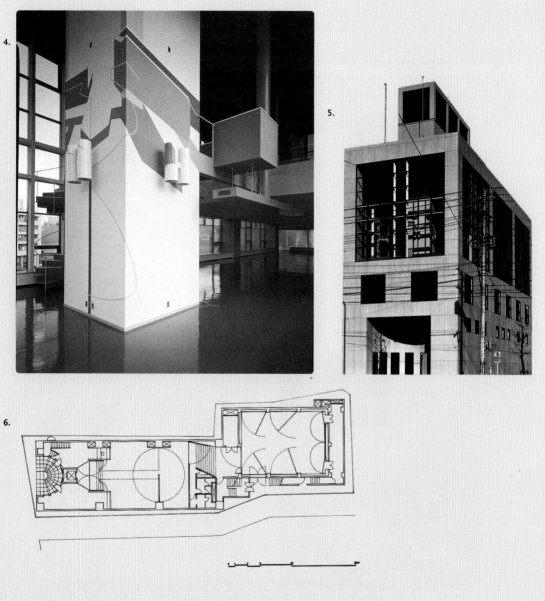

4. Painted shaft on fourth floor   **5.** Exterior view   **6.** First-floor plan

Main stair, showing the calculated dissolution of the physicality of the staircase

View looking west from the entrance hall across the gallery to the Japanese Art wing

View of the permanent exhibition gallery

The Museum of Modern Art, Gunma, Contemporary Art Wing

Twenty-five years after the opening of the Gunma museum, a contemporary art department and a new wing to house it have been added. The 12-cubic-meter frame of the original building was maintained, though a new treatment was created for the interior. There are now different solutions for each of the museum's collections. For classical art, the design of a case is emphasized; for modern art, the relationship between the work and the lighting is predominant; and for contemporary art, the focus is on the space generated by a work's installation in a gallery.

1. Inside of the high-side lighting of Exhibition space 5: Movable louvers and fluorescent lamps regulate the light

2. Exhibition space 5

3. Exhibition space 3: high-side lighting fixtures enable indirect light

1. Ground-floor connection to the Gunma Museum of History. An information center is under the new stair; beyond on the left is the museum shop.

2. Al fresco dining terrace under the Japanese Art wing, at its southwest corner

East extension from the southeast

KITA-KYUSHU CITY MUSEUM OF ART AND ANNEX

Kyta-kyushu, Fukuoka, Japan, 1972–74 and 1985–86 (annex)

The Kita-kyushu City Museum of Arts, located on a hilltop in the center of the city, has a commanding view of the surrounding area. One of its main purposes was to foster community pride, and it now stands as a distinctive monument and landmark.

The main gallery, completed in 1974, consists of two elongated cubes, 32 feet square on the face and 200 feet long. The two square faces seem to float out of the building, and the rest of the design has been submerged as much as possible to enhance this effect. Whereas the outer walls of the cubes are covered with four-foot-square die-cast aluminum panels, the lower part of the building, housing the other facilities, has walls of exposed concrete. This is to encourage ivy growth, which will eventually cloak the base of the structure in green, further accentuating the hovering cubes.

Beneath the cubes is the entrance hall, covered in white marble. To the left of the entrance is a naturally lit exhibition wing, and to the right is the office wing. An auditorium, a studio, and a small hall in the basement serve as a "living museum" for the community.

The annex was built to alleviate the space shortage in the main building, especially in the community galleries, and it stands to one side of the entrance court and main approach. The lower portion of the annex is of rusticated concrete, the upper portion is of brick. The first floor is an independent community gallery, and the second floor provides storage space and research areas. On the third-floor level are a sculpture garden, a gallery for woodblock prints, and an atrium that connects directly to the main gallery through an open corridor.

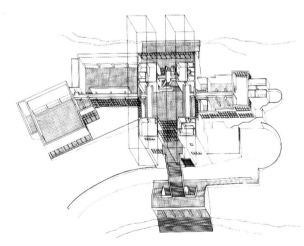

Axonometric, second-floor interior

Grand staircase

West view of annex building (left)

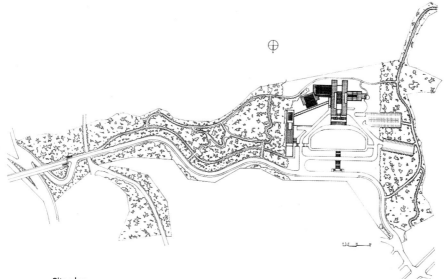

Site plan

Atrium

Terrace with *Utsurohi* by Aiko Miyawaki

Overall view

FUJIMI COUNTRY CLUBHOUSE

Oita, Japan, 1973–74

The question "Why do the Japanese love golf so much?"—often asked in Japan as well as elsewhere—is embodied in the plan of this golf clubhouse, which takes the shape of a question mark. The form was arrived at only in the final stage of design; the initial concept simply outlined a continuous barrel-vaulted structure. This was Isozaki's first use of the barrel vault, which appears again in several later designs. In the early 1970s he was working with the purest and most basic geometric forms, like the square, the circle, and the equilateral triangle, creating architecture by developing them into three dimensions. Here the barrel vault is reinterpreted in this spirit.

One reason for choosing a vault form was to secure the view over the golf course from inside the building. In terms of structure, this means that the vault must be supported with transverse tension bars to allow for windows in the walls beneath it. Sections that need to be closed off, like locker rooms, are set partially underground. Located above these are semi-independent spaces for the entrance hall, lounges, restaurant, meeting rooms, and other functions—developed in one almost continuous whole. It is the winding of the barrel-vault that makes it possible to create areas of spatial independence. The vault protrudes in front, forming a semicircular entrance canopy. The design of the front elevation includes references to the entrance section of Palladio's Villa Poiana.

Both exterior and interior walls are concrete faced with stucco. Sound-insulation plaster is sprayed onto the interior surface of the vault, while copper covers the roof on a base of thermal insulating material.

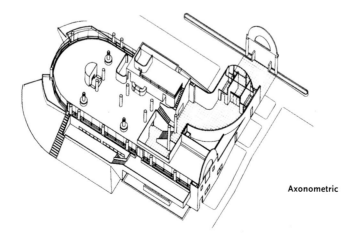

Axonometric

Exterior view, showing the barrel-vault roof

Lounge and dining hall

Interior detail

View of the clubhouse within the surrounding landscape

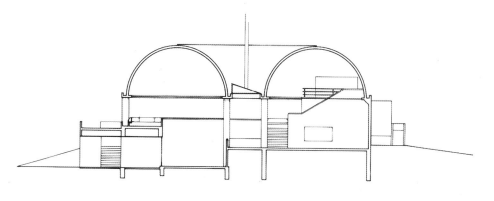

Section

Entrance

KITA-KYUSHU CENTRAL LIBRARY

Kita-kyushu, Fukuoka, Japan, 1973–74

This project, which came directly after the Fujimi Country Clubhouse, also features a big, double-barrel-vault roof. The program called for an independent cultural facility housing the city's central library, a historical museum, and an audiovisual resource center, all combined on one site. The scheme gathers all of these elements within one architectural form, unified by the barrel vaults.

In one short section the two vaulted roofs run parallel. One soon turns away from its partner, and then turns in on itself again, while the other continues on in the same direction, ending in a short "hook." The first vault covers the historical museum; the second tops the library and, in its hook, the audiovisual center. The barrel vaults are composed of two precast-concrete panels connected to each other at the central top section, forming three-pin arches, covered by copper sheets. Three kinds of precast-concrete forms are used for the roof base—one for linear parts and two fan shapes for curved parts—and the top line of the vault is horizontally supported. The height of the rooms underneath is adjusted for various levels

using base sections of cast-in-place concrete, resulting in rooms in a wide range of sizes. The precast ribs are left exposed, and the rhythmical articulation of rooms is visible in the ceilings.

Parallel to the gradually rising floor levels in the library building is an interior sloping path. Forming an L shape, the long rear elevation faces onto a park, and the approach by foot to the building is on this side. From the other side of the library building the keep of the town castle can be seen.

The museum is devoted to exhibitions of ancient dwellings and other structures of the region, as well as of historical materials relating to the area's culture. At one end of the museum is a large stained-glass "rose window" designed by Isozaki. It is a colorful representation of a diagram—created by the philosopher Baien Miura, who was born nearby—that expresses the ideas of the cosmos and nature in terms of the Oriental concept of yin and yang. The restaurant facing it has an external form determined by Isozaki's "Marilyn Monroe" curve. These elements serve as a contrast to the historical architectural forms of the vaults and the rose window.

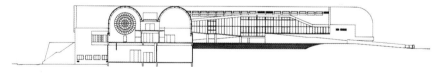

East—west section

View from the street, showing the curved barrel-vault roof

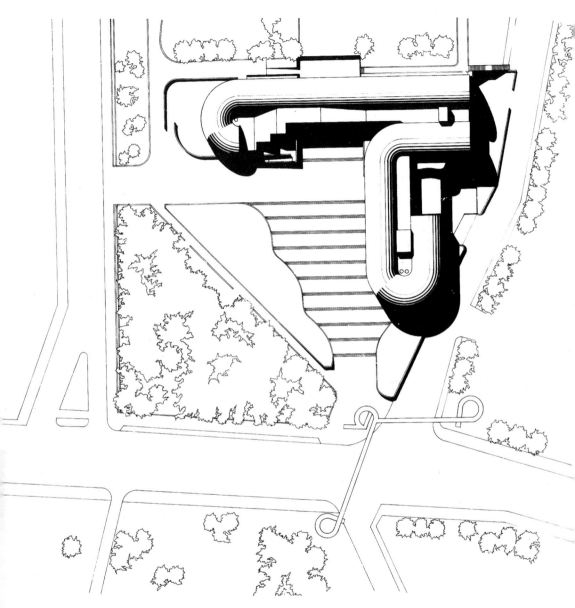

Site plan

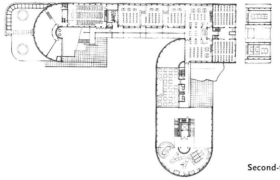

Second-floor plan

West view of museum block

The rose window from inside

Southeast view

KAMIOKA TOWN HALL

Kamioka, Gifu, Japan, 1976–78

The initial plan for this building, to be located in the middle of the remote mining town of Kamioka, was for a rather low structure that would remain inconspicuous among the surrounding houses, with their tarred tin roofs. This design was rejected, however, and a building that contrasted with the dark atmosphere of the town was requested instead. The final design is a structure that resembles a spaceship with an exterior of gleaming silver aluminum.

Several basic forms are combined in this building, which also has an unusual combination of finishing materials (aluminum and granite). The cubic structure of the main entrance for the executive offices is faced in pink granite. A double-cylinder form houses the reception area on the lower floor and an assembly hall on the upper floor. The area in between, in certain respects an extension of the entrance block, is used for offices; Isozaki's "Marilyn Monroe" curve provides a softening effect here.

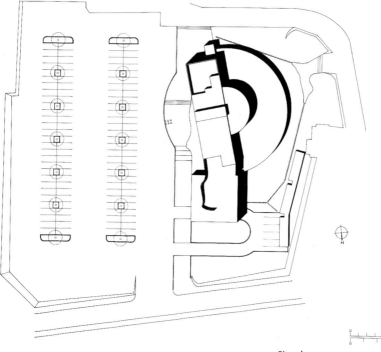

Site plan

Exterior view of the assembly hall, with offices underneath

Public gallery on fourth floor

Lobby on first floor

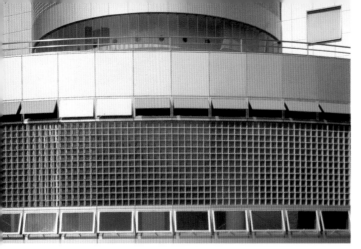

Detail of the exterior

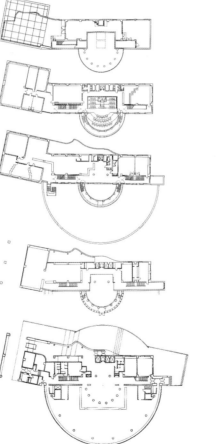

Fifth-floor plan

Fourth-floor plan

Third-floor plan

Second-floor plan

First-floor plan

Overall view

CONCEPTUAL PROPOSAL: Electric Labyrinth (Ruins Drawing)

1968

The installation, created for the fourteenth Milan Triennale, was divided into two sections: a maze of sixteen revolving, curved Plexiglas panels, and a huge screen onto which images were cast by three projectors.

The screen was printed with photographs of the devastated, charred remains of Hiroshima after the bomb was dropped; projected onto it, creating a contextual montage, were images of building ruins from cities of the future—brilliant, optimistic visions from the proposals created by Japanese architects in the early 1960s. The projects seemed to say that the fate awaiting all planning proposals, even those that are realized, is one of obliteration, just like Hiroshima.

The revolving panels carried a variety of images: people trapped in urban environments, glimpses of the abused and misused in Japan, visions of hell, late Edo *ukiyo-e* prints, bombed human bodies, urchins, wastrels, and ghosts. The panels were rotated manually or by signals from an infrared beam; either way, viewers were implicated in their activation.

Ruins of Hiroshima, "Electric Labyrinth," 1968

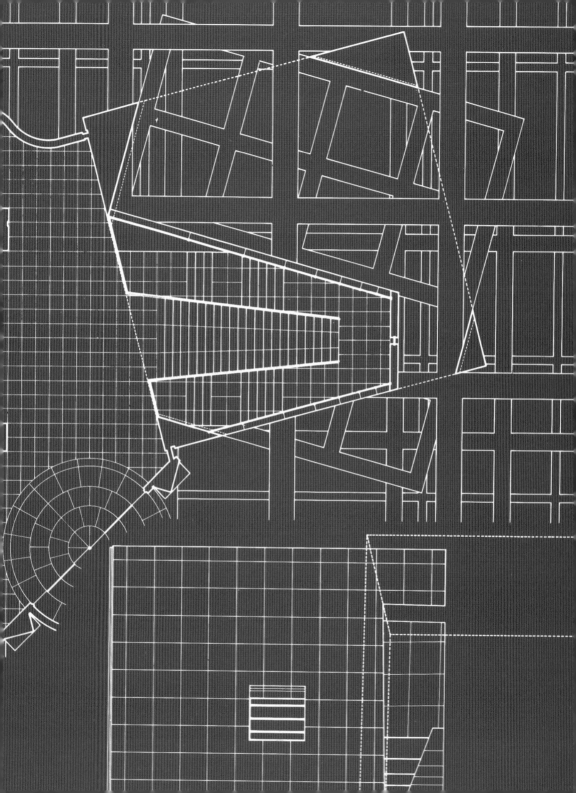

1980s: Narrative

STYLE IN RUINS: TIME AND SPACE = TIME AND HISTORY

During the 1980s I was in my fifties. Although I have said that I experience some kind of crisis every decade, during this period, with an architectural office to operate and constant work to do, I could not afford to take to my bed. Even without a severe crisis, I underwent a change in methodology that gave a new aspect to the *maniera* doctrine I propounded during the 1970s. In terms of political metaphor, throughout the 1960s I advocated a guerrilla-like destructive operation, the major theme of which was criticism of Modernist architecture. Our generation came to be called the "Dissolution Generation," from the title of one of my books, *Kenchiko no kaitai* (The Dissolution of Architecture).

The philosophy firmly formulated by Modernist architecture fused function and form, advocating a kind of utopian progress, and gave rise to the so-called International Style, which was supposed to be universal. I, however, felt that all of this should be broken down and that reconstruction should begin from the point at which architectural discourse had been reduced to zero. My doctrine of *maniera*, influenced by Russian formalism, was an attempt to put the automatic movement of forms at the core of architectural method. My strategy was to isolate architectural discourse from politics and society with the idea that an apolitical stance would become political.

The theories formulated on the rectilinear, utopian idea of progress that underpinned Modernist architecture look like the kind of dissolution I mentioned earlier. In fact, however, those theories represented contextualism in the wider sense. Each place has its own physical, daily life and cultural context. Since they are often evaluated on the extent to which they suit the context, new buildings are supposed to harmonize with existing patterns.

However, in my opinion, finding reliable urban contexts in Japan constitutes a major difficulty. I therefore believe that new buildings should stimulate the creation of new contexts in their surroundings. This is why my buildings assume either an aggressive or a defensive posture in relation to their settings.

In other words, my doctrine of *maniera* is anti-contextualist. My buildings are expected to generate discord with their settings. Suddenly a town hall that looks like a spaceship seems to have floated down into what had been a peaceful town. One of my buildings suggests a great whale swirling about at the base of a traditional castle. Another looks like a grounded sailing vessel. These and my bright red walls cutting through a pastoral setting are all alien elements that throw their environments into confusion.

The *maniera* method achieves transformations because once the struggle with the location is over, direct confrontation with the broader culture behind it becomes possible. In 1978 I developed this theme in the exhibition, "*Ma*, Japanese Time-Space." The concept of *ma*, or interval, for which we Japanese require no explanation, pervades our lives and our art in general, as well as our feelings, methods, and artistic awareness. For the sake of people from the West I attempted to explain it according to Western logic as far as possible. Elements presented in the exhibition included painting, sculpture, music, dramatic performance, gardening, architecture, poetry, and daily life, along with the Japanese language essential to it. An oblique line traversing these elements was drawn and explained by means of objects, sounds, actions, and words. Oddly enough, during this process, the theories I had considered peculiarly Japanese dissolved. In other words, when the Western world was superimposed on the Japanese, a gap was generated and deconstruction automatically occurred.

The Tsubuka Center building, designed immediately after this 1978 Paris exhibition, represents my attempt to deconstruct Western elements by means of Japanese elements. Tsukuba was the sole new town project by the Japanese government after World War II. The Tsukuba Center building is a complex facility. In its design I referred to the classical tradition of the West. The details in which these classical references were embodied eliminated all traces of a unifying system that might extend outward to the whole. Consequently, the elements quoted from heterogeneous sources overlap in a fragmented way. I refer to this ironically as schizophrenic eclecticism. My approach in this instance can be said to resemble the way traditional Japanese architecture and garden designs evade totalizing systems by employing noncompositional, nonhierarchical compositional principles. Looking back, I see that the Tsukuba Center design is a mixture of classical precedents, Modernist elements, and references to my own past works. In it, however, my most profound concern was the disjunctive placing of elements.

The Tsukuba Center's central plaza is sunken. Deciding to use a sunken area was another step toward avoiding an overall totalizing system. In addition, it implies political metaphor: by eliminating the element that should hint at its presence, I created a void at the heart of a place that should have been a stage for the Japanese nation. Whereas during the 1970s I had appeared all the more political by refraining from political discussion, at this point I found myself in a position where connections with politics were forced upon me. I used irony to deal with this situation—eliminating the center—though

I only did so as a result of being placed in confrontation with the nation.

In the case of the design for The Museum of Contemporary Art in Los Angeles, I confronted political elements from the very outset. The city of Los Angeles is located at a point of confluence between the culture of the East and the West. Inevitably an Asian architect called to work there must provide a methodological interpretation of both cultures. To satisfy this demand, I refined my design approach into a homage to the golden section, as the Western method of establishing divisions, and the yin and yang philosophy, as the corresponding Eastern method. From my experience superimposing the Western and the Japanese to generate gaps for interpretation and construction, I was able to design in an ambivalent way, to produce something that is neither oriental nor occidental while being both. During the process, I myself was drawn into a vortex of examination and interpretation arising from the collision of heterogeneous cultures.

I used a central sunken patio and housed the galleries in two flanking wings apportioned on the golden section. This composition creates a vortex, which stimulates a flow that has been treated similarly to the excursion path that plays an important role in many traditional Japanese-garden designs. This simultaneously realized both Eastern and Western spatial divisions.

The architectural forms projecting above ground are based on Platonic solids but at the same time allude to such historical precedents as the pyramids, Palladio, the palazzo, and so on. Juxtaposing the abstract and the concrete, the modern and the classical, and hard and smooth materials results in ambivalence. Nothing is clearly quoted as a source, nor did I intend to revive any single style. Instead, my aim was to dismantle apparently integrated architectural styles and to fragment them so that, at the moment when they seem to be in ruins, a schizophrenic state of suspension is created. The fragments lose their points of origin. Dispersed as forms, shapes, elements, and pieces devoid of meaning in contemporary time, they flash on and off through metaphor. The effective method in this case is assembling fragments, as in a collage or a patchwork quilt.

Under such circumstances all architectural style is reduced to ruins. The only things available for architectural design are the fragments scattered in the ruins. Should reconstruction be accomplished, the results would no doubt still resemble ruins. This is why architecture must become schizophrenic and eclectic. The art of assembling fragments in a given place to intersect with the local context is political in nature. Consequently, architecture may well have to be reinterpreted on the basis of political significance. When this happens, architecture will find itself under a new program of discourse.

ARATA ISOZAKI

TSUKUBA CENTER BUILDING

Tsukuba Science City, Ibaragi, Japan, 1979–83

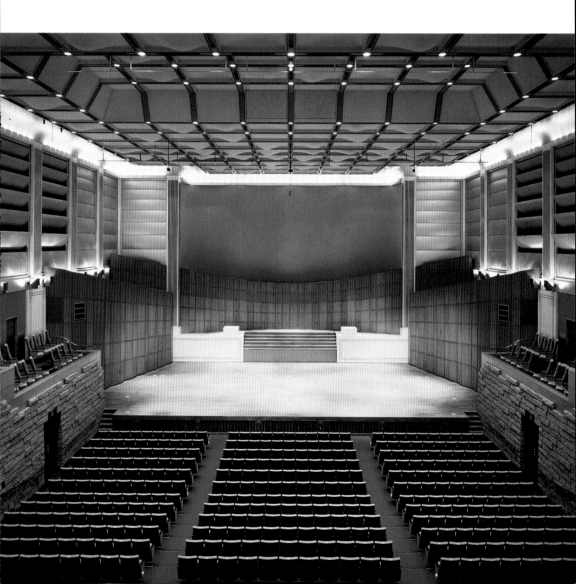

Tsukuba Science City, located forty miles from Tokyo, is a unique phenomenon in Japan. The planners' intention was to centralize in Tsukuba various university and government research facilities that had been scattered throughout Tokyo. But what sets Tsukuba apart from other large-scale "new towns" built in Japanese suburbs after the war is the fact that, along with housing, it provides many of the amenities associated with urban life.

The Tsukuba Center Building was designed as a civic center complex to bring life and activity to the city. It includes a hotel, a concert hall, an information center, a shopping mall, and a community center.

The planning of the town is characterized by its circulation system, in which interconnected pedestrian decks bridge over the vehicular traffic routes at ground level. These bridges provide pedestrian access to the Tsukuba Center Building, located on the primary north-south axis of the town. One level below the pedestrian decks is the focus of the complex, a sunken plaza or "forum," whose design is essentially a reverse quotation of the Campidoglio in Rome.

A concert hall and an information center with audiovisual equipment occupy the south block of the building, with shops

arranged around the sunken plaza. The east block consists of two cubes. The larger one houses the hotel and contains the entrance hall on the first floor, a restaurant and coffee shop on the second, and banquet halls of various sizes on the third and fourth. The fifth through tenth floors hold the guest rooms, and the top floor contains a sky lounge and a restaurant. The smaller cube, which has been rotated off the plaza's axis and sliced off on one corner, is a separate banquet hall.

On the sides of the building that face vehicular traffic zones, the exterior is relatively simple and unarticulated, while the sides facing the plaza display a wide variety of forms and finishes. Here the ground floor is rusticated, using locally quarried granite and artificial stone. The upper parts of the building are clad in silver tile—with glazed and unglazed pieces forming a pattern—and aluminum panels, which are used to cover curved surfaces or to highlight specific parts. Geometric shapes—triangles, semicircles, cubes, cylinders—are found on the facade, as are references to traditional architectural forms like columns and arch details. No single, organized system defines or unifies the overall design; each element has its own distinctive character.

The interior of the concert hall

The east facade from the parking area

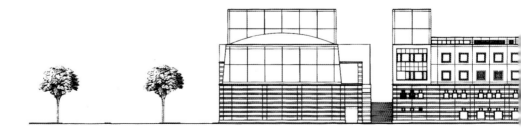

The plaza amphitheater

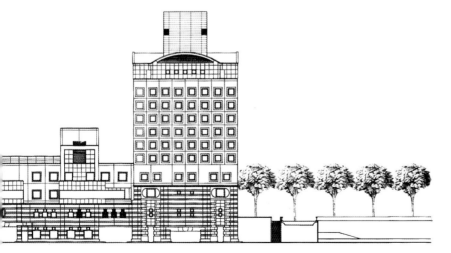

LEFT Elevation of the concert hall and RIGHT the hotel

View from the sunken plaza

Outdoor stage elements

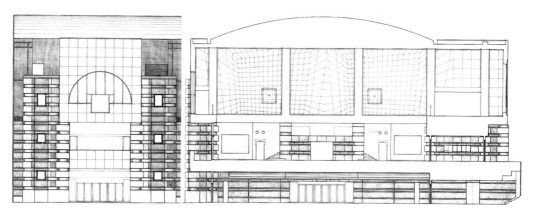

Facade detail

Detail of the lighting in the banquet hall

Detail of the exterior finish

ART TOWER MITO

Mito, Ibaragi, Japan, 1986–90

Detail of ceiling of the conference hall

The Art Tower Mito occupies a block in the old part of Mito, one street away from the old highway that passes east to west through the city. More than half of the site is to be given over to an urban square, and the facility itself is designed as a townscape around the square. It is a small redevelopment project from the point of view of Mito as a whole, but this urban environment is intended to be a new cultural core that will stimulate the reorganization of the surrounding area, away from the linear development along the highway.

The new complex is arranged around the square, which has a green that is open to the public day and night. It includes a 330-foot-high symbolic tower (100 meters, commemorating Mito's centennial), a theater, a concert hall, and a gallery of contemporary art. Although drama, music, and art activities are accommodated in separate facilities, the spaces are close to one another and have a common area so that interrelationships can develop across different fields. The theater and the concert hall are located along the western street, and between them is the entrance hall for the entire complex, which is equipped with a pipe organ. On the northern street, behind a cascade on the square, are offices, curatorial rooms, a restaurant (on the first floor), and the gallery (on the second). A two-story conference hall is located on the southwestern corner of the square. Underground facilities include rehearsal and dressing rooms, art-storage space, and a 250-car parking garage.

The square is accessible from all directions. One passes under three large oaks (on the south side), alongside the symbolic tower (the east), behind the cascade (the north), or through the entrance hall (the west).

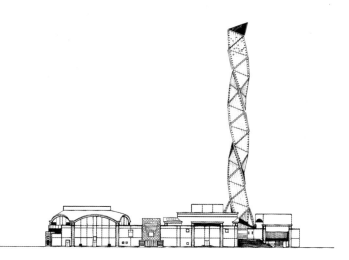

West elevation

One gallery opens to the next

View of the tower from between the theater and the concert hall

Exterior of the gallery

The tower at night

THE MUSEUM OF CONTEMPORARY ART, LOS ANGELES

Los Angeles, California, 1981–86

The Museum of Contemporary Art (MOCA) is located at the center of the California Plaza mixed-use development in the Bunker Hill section of downtown Los Angeles. Although California Plaza was realized in stages, MOCA was bounded by an office tower on the south, residential condominiums on the east, and Grand Avenue on the west. The museum sits atop and partially within the parking structure of the plaza.

Along with 24,500 square feet of exhibition space, the museum building includes an auditorium, a library, a café, a bookstore, and office and support areas, which are located on different levels.

The museum presents itself to the street as two structures bracketing a sculpture court and a lower entry court. Pyramids, cubes, and a semicircular vault rest atop walls of red Indian sandstone on a base of red granite. Bands of polished sandstone alternate with bands of larger, rusticated pieces to create a subtle pattern of horizontal situations. On the north, the copper-sheathed vaulted library bridges over the pedestrian path, forming a symbolic gateway to the museum. Beneath this gateway is a green aluminum-clad cube that houses the ticket booth. On the south

are three pyramids: the large pyramid, whose lower portion is clad in copper, serves as a skylight for the entrance gallery, while the small pyramids provide illumination for one of the exhibition galleries. Eight more small pyramids, as well as twelve linear skylights, allow natural light into other galleries.

The sculpture court, which overlooks the entry court below, is the focus of the various museum facilities that open onto the plaza level, including the bookstore and the office lobby. From the sculpture court visitors descend the grand stair to the entry court, which gives access to the galleries. This sunken entry allows for maximum ceiling heights in the exhibition areas while conforming to the height limitations of California Plaza. The entry court, the lobby, and the café are finished in the same materials—floors of granite, walls of white crystallized glass and sandstone—creating the impression of one open, continuous space.

Within the museum the galleries are characterized by variations in proportion, shape, and quality of light, both natural and artificial.

View from the entrance hall

View from the plaza level

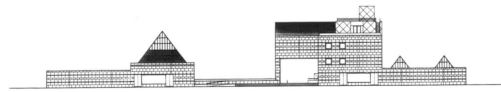

East elevation

REFERENCE: Hara Museum ARC

There were two special conditions that had to be met in the design of the summer annex to the Hara Museum Arc, which is on a ranch about two hours outside of Tokyo. One, it is the only museum in greater Tokyo specializing in contemporary art at the present. Consequently, it could be open during only part of the year. Two, performances such as outdoor concerts had to be accommodated because the ranch is not only a working farm but a tourist-oriented facility as well. Moreover, the director of the museum is active not only in the promotion of international artistic activities, but in the lumber business, so from the start the building was expected to be constructed of wood.

1.

2.

3.

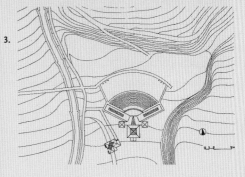

1. Main facade with approach and amphitheater   **2.** Overall view   **3.** Site plan

4.

5.

4. Gallery C, detail of natural and
artificial lighting

5. Detail of skylighting

View of a gallery space

THE MUSEUM OF CONTEMPORARY ART, LOS ANGELES

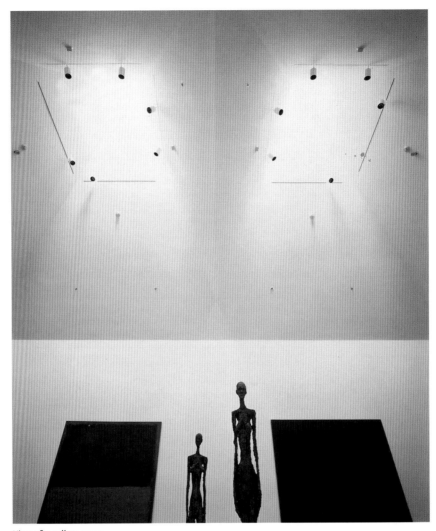

View of a gallery space

Section

Pyramidal skylights

Interior stairs

View of a gallery space

SANT JORDI SPORTS HALL

Montjuic, Barcelona, Spain, 1983–90

This sports hall was designed as one of the central facilities at Montjuic, the main event area for the 1992 Olympics in Barcelona.

The sports hall was planned to include an ice hockey rink, a 200-meter track, and other sports facilities; it can also accommodate concerts, conventions, exhibitions, and other non-sports uses. Spectators enter the hall from the square on the north side; athletes, service staff, and press approach from the street on the south side, where the level is fifty feet lower than the north entrance. Between the main arena and the secondary arenas are circulation areas, locker rooms, dressing rooms, restaurants, and offices.

The hall is covered with a double-layer, dome-shaped space frame whose construction was specially designed: three hinged sections are jointed horizontally and assembled in a folded state on the ground before being raised in the air and fixed in their final shape. The roof makes reference to the mountain on which the building is situated; soaring 148 feet above the arena floor at its highest point, it provides the structure with an airiness that is often lacking in similar sports halls. Perforated-metal screens allow for light control within the space frame. Brick, stone, tile, zinc, and other local materials have been used in a variety of ways for the interior and exterior finishes.

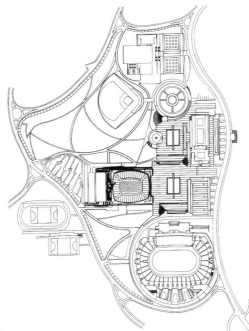

Site plan

Exterior view, under construction

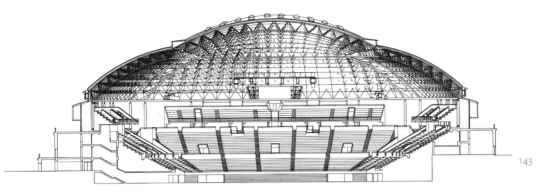

Transverse section

143

Interior view, with the pin-jointed columns

Entrance plaza, with *Utsurohi* by Aiko Miyawaki

Corridor

TEAM DISNEY BUILDING

Lake Buena Vista, Florida, 1987–90

Walt Disney World, just outside Orlando, Florida, is on a vast site of 29,000 acres, an area twice the size of Manhattan. Walt Disney's dream was to construct a model of the city of the future here; theme parks such as the Magic Kingdom, EPCOT Center, and Disney/MGM Studios have already been built on the site.

Disney Village, the area near the main entrance to Walt Disney World from the freeway, is the site for the headquarters of Disney Florida Operating Divisions, collected in a single building.

With a total length of 820 feet on a north-south axis, the building is divided into three blocks. Almost all office functions are contained in two long north and south four-story blocks of identical design. Each block is laterally divided by an atrium on the central axis. Skylights on the office-block roofs allow daylight to pour into this interior/exterior space; bridges and stairways provide connections across the divide. Aluminum and reflective glass are flush on the curtain wall, creating a smooth, continuous exterior.

Between the two wings is the entrance lobby, an ensemble of forms grouped around a huge truncated cone. The cone, 120 feet in diameter at its base and 120 feet high, stands as the functional and visual focus of atten-tion, inviting people into the building. The long axis of the entrance is turned slightly off the central axis, breaking up the longitudinal mass of the office blocks. A variety of materials, colors, patterns, shapes, and structures in this area provide distinctive accents to the architecture. The walls colliding with the cone are blue, and red cube skylights are inserted into the roof of the entrance block. A huge stylus atop the cone throws shadows into the interior space, forming a sundial indicating the time and season. Check patterns in two types of red granite are used to cover two other elements of the entrance block, one containing an entrance hall, the other a conference room at the third-floor level. Access to this conference room is provided by a bridge passing through the cone. The main entrance to the building is covered by a "Mickey" canopy that pierces the cube leading directly into the open courtyard in the cone.

The building straddles the east end of an artificial lake, a prominent feature of the landscaping. The lake surface, the architectural composition, and the color scheme combine to establish the presence of this flagship building at the forefront of Walt Disney World.

Central block from west

View from east

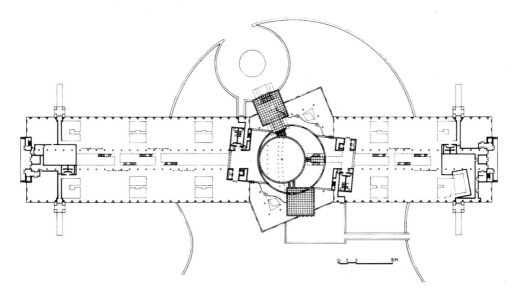

First-floor plan

Sundial court

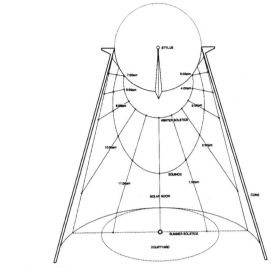

Conceptual diagram of the sundial

West facade with pond

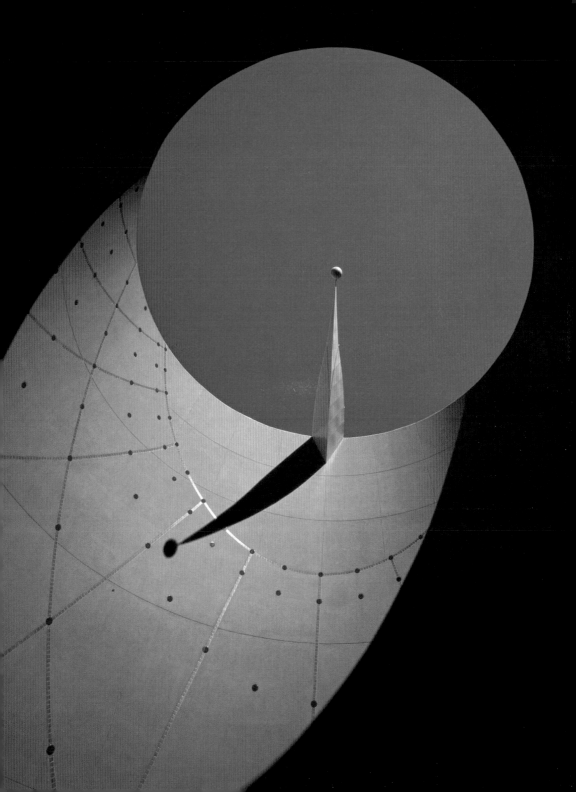

CONCEPTUAL PROPOSAL: New Tokyo City Hall

In need of a new metropolitan government building for a three-block site amidst the skyscraper slabs west of Shinjuku Station, the city held an invitational competition for a facility to replace the seriously overextended building in Marunouchi. Despite the division of the site into two blocks on one side of the street and one on the other side, the competition specifications seemed to call for a design that was, as much as possible, integrated into a single structure. This would both establish the presence of the new city hall within its imposing surroundings and improve the efficiency of administrative operations. In response to the program, this scheme has a somewhat independent international conference center and an open area occupying one block, with administration offices and the Metropolitan Assembly on the two blocks across the street.

Model of the proposal among the neighboring high rises; view of southwest

Model, view of north

Longitudinal section, silk-screen

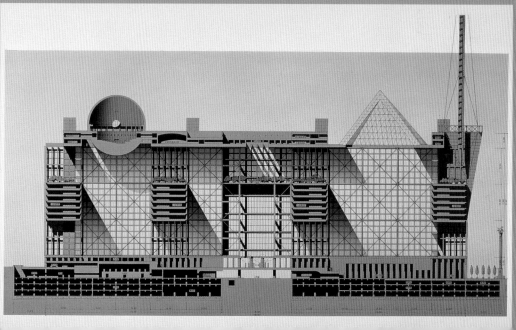

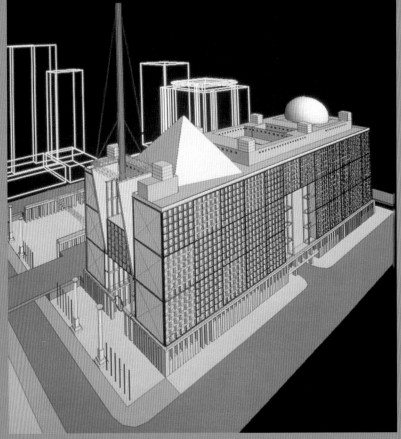

Computer graphic, exterior perspective

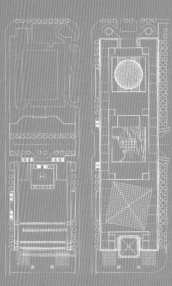

Site plan

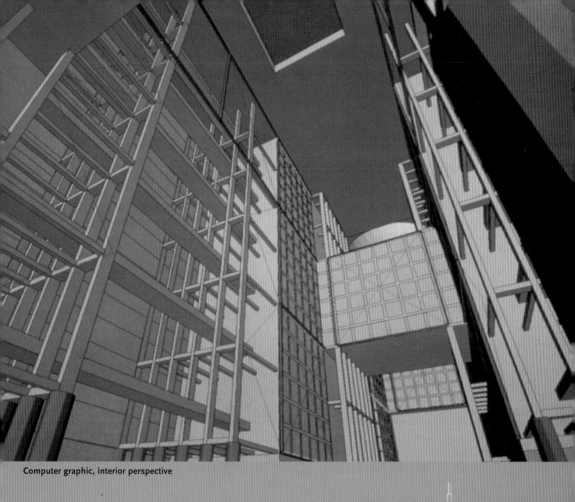

Computer graphic, interior perspective

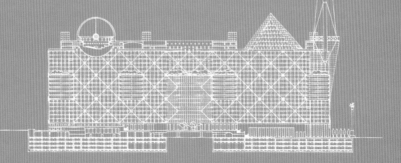

Longitudinal section

NEW TOKYO CITY HALL

This project is part of redevelopment plans for the Ueno Railway Station, one of the main terminals in Tokyo for suburban and intercity trains. The proposed redevelopment focuses on improving the station itself and strengthening its functions. The program calls for a 1.1 million-square-foot hotel, a 900,000-square-foot department store, a theater, an art gallery, and additions and extensions to reconfigure the interior of the station. The total floor area will comprise 2.8 million square feet.

1.

2.

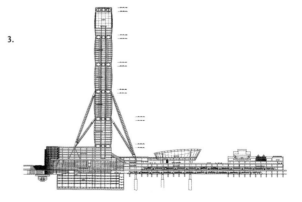

3.

1. Model, proposal, 1991   **2.** Superimposed aerial photograph   **3.** Section, proposal, 1991

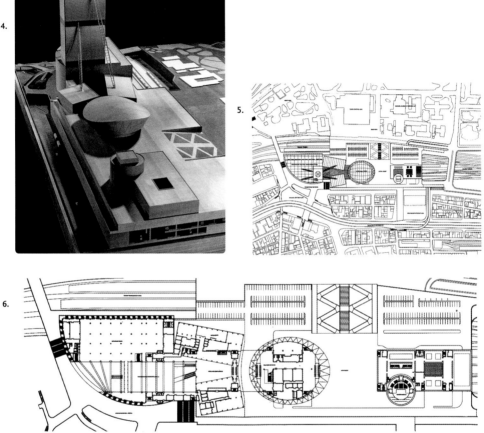

4. Model, proposal, 1991   **5.** Site plan, proposal, 1991   **6.** Fifth-floor plan, proposal, 1991

1990s: Form

The twelve zodiac signs of Eastern astrology represent the cycles of a person's life. *Kanreki* is the completion of five cycles, culminating in the sixtieth birthday, and it is believed that the next life then begins. At age sixty, people experience a so-called second birth.

When I was reaching *kanreki*, a retrospective of my architectural work, *Arata Isozaki: Architecture 1960–1990*, was mounted at the Museum of Contemporary Art, Los Angeles. (It later traveled around the around, and an earlier edition of the current book was published by Rizzoli as a catalogue for that show.) I organized the exhibition so as to encapsulate all of my past work. I associated the circulation through the exhibition with Eastern astrology, privately hoping to enact the ritual of my own rebirth.

The exhibition documented thirty works, built and unbuilt, from thirty years. Each was presented in three parallel descriptive dimensions: as a realized, life-size building; as a wooden model; and as descriptions of "constructed form." The presentation was intended to show how each work was an *écriture* that targeted "architecture" as a meta-concept. I sought to conceptualize the cycle of "architecture" in its entirety: I posited architecture at the terminus of a life cycle. This was, in a way, however, putting the cart before the horse. The normal sequence would have been first to assimilate the Western concept of architecture and then begin a practice from it, but in Japan, where Western concepts had not been fully adopted, architecture was never spoken of positively, even in the mid-twentieth century, when modernism was already well established—and seemingly acclimated to the native culture—in our country.

At the outset of my practice, geometry and new technological ideas were my guides. Geometric concepts become objects when they are spatially concretized, as do technological achievements. But, then, what makes these objects architecture? In my thirty years of practice, I had consistently sought the often simple procedure that transforms objects into architecture. The electronic robot (Expo '70/Festival Plaza), the cubic frame (The Museum of Modern Art, Gunma), a wave of quoted signs (Tsukuba Center Building), the tetrahedron (Art Tower Mito), the sundial (Team Disney Building)—

these are all outside historically acknowledged architectural language. In designing the projects, I intended to make these outsiders into architecture. Not everyone appreciated my procedures, and I cannot explain every one of them, but I have insisted that there must be a proper procedure if architecture as metaconcept exists beyond the material level.

However, in the West, as in Japan, architecture was abandoned at the dawn of modernity because of the burden of historical memory. At this time in Japan, where modernism was introduced later than in the West, architecture was simply absent. Although the causes—abandonment and absence—of this lack were different in the West and in Japan, the loss of architectural discourse vis-à-vis architecture was shared. In the late 1980s I encountered a number of architects from various movements who felt the need to reposition architecture as the base of their practices. Now, during the 1990s, I have been involved in the international annual conference ANY, which addresses the problems of architecture that I encounter in my practice: undecidability, conceptual architecture, semiotic space, virtual reality, and so on.

"Architecture" is a transcendental concept that functions purely as "constructed form" or a "device for becoming." I have identified Demiurge in Plato's *Timaeus* as the earliest prototype of this function, and I have come to call the genesis of this function "Demiurgomorphism." I have conceived Demiurge—who alters, by his reckless interventions, the mechanism of universal becoming—as a model for architecture based on the measure of the human body and as the basis for all classical thought and aestheticism. I came to consider architecture as the art of Demiurge, and having sealed together my thirty-year practice in an exhibition, my new objective has been to recover the art of Demiurge.

Between the Chinese cultural revolution in 1968 and the collapse of the Berlin wall in 1989, the world was suspended in a nuclear threat of opposing superpowers. The world was frozen, and it was impossible to consider culture and art within the political situation. After the Chinese cultural revolution, I sought to make architecture totally autonomous. By eliminating all sociopolitical elements, I left architecture to pursue its purest state through the autonomous deployment of form. I withdrew from urbanism, my main concern in the 1960s. I shunned not only urban planning, but also the consideration of the urban context in architecture. Stripping away all external influences allowed the autonomous movement of form to lead everything else. Within this framework, even works of historical architecture, which had evolved over time, were deemed quotable references. My theoretical inquiry into architecture—from procedure (*shuho-ron*) to semiotic rhetoric (*shuji-ron*)—was constructed as a discourse during this time of suspension. My consistent point was that it was impossible for politics—as a grand narrative constructed by opposing forces—to affect architecture; the only possible reciprocity between them was irony.

The sudden release of this suspension of history has shaken nations around the world. Big nations crumbled because of their inability to control power/information, while borders were easily trespassed by the media network. Thus arose various micro-conflicts. Consequently, neither actual building sites nor architectural discourse could avoid the sociopolitics caused by this conjuncture. Nuclear weapons, which had been stockpiled in a few arsenals, were redistributed throughout the world, creating a renewed awareness of holocausts. At the same time, the rights of the weak, which had been repressed by collective power, were now resurrected. Gender, race, class, disability, victimization, pollution, lost memories—all of these "minor" elements returned as subjects of architectural discourse. The politicization of architecture was evident: the politics of form replaced the semantics of morphology.

The political is the very metaphor for undecidability, the ground for all of today's architectural discourses. In the determination of architectural design, there is no single absolute answer. Undecidability stubbornly drones on. Finally, however, a decision is forced by the intervention of the political. It is now impossible to construct architecture as an autonomous entity, especially after the end of the Cold War. A single subjective judgment cannot constitute the solution to the architectural problematic. If a solution can be achieved at all, it is only by an open system that accommodates manifold others.

For this reason, I have decided to take on, in addition to my own architectural projects, the role of producer for projects whose resolutions can be achieved only through collaboration.

Many younger architects contributed to the Nexus World Project (1991)[1] and Kumamoto Artpolis (1988–),[2] in which a common urban space has been constructed. The Japanese Pavilion at the Sixth Venice Biennale International Exhibition of Architecture (1996),[3] which received the Leon d'Or prize, showed how a city dies and is reborn by representing the Hanshin Awaji earthquake disaster through photographs and actual rubble from the site.

In *Visions of Japan* (1991),[4] an exhibition at the Victoria & Albert Museum, three Japanese architects—Toyoo Itoh, Osamu Ishiyama, and Kazuhiro Ishii—presented idiosyncratically the "game sensibility" of Japanese daily life.

As a juror for the Minamata Memorial Competition (1996) to commemorate the victims of organic mercury poisoning,[5] I was concerned with establishing a place of repose for the victims' souls, as well as preserving the memory of the tragedy.

I commissioned only female architects and artists for the design of the public housing of Gifu Kitagata Apartments (1998).[6] In doing so, I intended both to criticize the male-oriented principle of public-housing projects in Japan and, more generally, to consider gender in the design of public spaces.

The construction of disaster memorials (for earthquakes, environmental pollution, etc.), the sense of game and communality in daily life, engagement with the issue of gender—these are the problematics of the 1990s that architects can no longer avoid. Furthermore, they are political on both the micro and macro scales. The construction of these problematics today yields architecture of the highest order, but simple individual intervention no longer suffices. Collaboration is now required. It is essential to construct a design process that allows the intervention of many voices.

In *"Haishi": Mirage City—Another Utopia,*[7] an exhibition at the Intercommunication Center Gallery in Tokyo, I presented a simulation of a city's becoming in which others intervene incessantly. As information from the outside was collected from the internet, transforming the design prototype, twelve visiting architects and artists participated with their sequential proposals, exhibiting one after another and responding to the previous proposal in the manner of *renga*, the Japanese traditional verse that employs a collaborative, participatory manner.

I have become a producer in an attempt to concretize the art of Demiurge. Due to the intervention of unidentifiable others in the architectonic, one must now anticipate the dynamism created by contingency and uncertainty.

To further this idea, in the early 1990s I began to critically recategorize building types by examining the various functions of cultural institutions. My initial motivation was to transform the types of my previous work—an object as enclosed system—into open systems by introducing historicity, social roles, and the structure of institutions.

I have called the Nagi Museum of Contemporary Art (1991–94) a museum of the third generation of contemporary art. If the first generation is "appropriation art" and the second "community art," the third will be "public art" centered on installation. My intention toward the architectonic was to create a place in which installation and architecture become one, a museum wherein the temporary event is permanently exhibited in a public space. Thus I collaborated with three artists—Aiko Miyawaki, Shusaku Arakawa, and Kazuo Okazaki—who are engaged in totally different spatial orientations. This design proposes one solution to today's situation, when museums are no longer able to accommodate new types of artwork.

The Toyonokuni Library for Cultural Resources (1991–95) introduced a new system of preserving and presenting the image of electronic media and information science. A large reading room, called the space of one hundred columns (*hyaku chu-no-ma*), assumes a constantly changing spatial arrangement; it consists of eighty-one cubic units with one hundred pillars.

While the Kyoto Concert Hall (1991–95) used the rectangular-type as its basic frame, in accord with the competition regulations, Nara Convention Hall (1992) introduces a transformative mechanism of audience seating: the space metamorphoses from a "virtual" stage (*kyo-butai*) to an arena to an end stage. In the Akiyoshidai International Arts Village, located in a region with many caves, floating concert stages in the hall are a metaphor for the caves. This new type of concert space, tailored to the repertoires and the styles of performance, is totally unprecedented.

In the 1970s, my design process involved extracting elementary units from primary shapes—the cubic frame from the square, the barrel vault from the circle. The interaction of these two elements directed my designs. Similarly, in the 1990s, the most important interaction in my practice is between two series: one based on the cubic unit with a full range of columns and one based on the shell surface with clothoid curve. This correspondence of design methods across decades is a result of my studio methodology: linguistic articulation and restriction of architectonic morphosis. To generate a shell surface with clothoid curve, complex geometry is subjected to computer analysis, but analytical methods are being developed that can easily draw much more complex surfaces, which tend to liquidize the hitherto enclosed geometric object. I call this new direction "undulation morphosis," and the beginnings of it can be seen in the roof of the Japanese Art and Technology Center in Kraków (1990–94). When all the works in this book are complete, this direction will be revealed as dominant in my work.

ARATA ISOZAKI

1. Nexus World Project, Fukuoka City, Japan, 1991. For a group of mid-rise collective dwelling units, Arata Isozaki & Associates served as the coordinator and invited six architects—Oscar Tusquets, Christian de Portzamparc, Osamu Ishiyama, Mark Mac, Rem Koolhaas, and Steven Holl—to propose new designs that would alter the inhabitants' daily lives.

2. Kumamoto Artpolis, Kumamoto Prefecture, Japan, 1988– . Sponsored by Kumamoto Prefecture, this enterprise, on which I served as commissioner from 1988–98, intends to leave an architectural legacy to future generations. It has already resulted in the realization of more than fifty projects.

3. Sixth Venice Biennale International Exhibition of Architecture, Venice, Italy, September 15–November 17, 1996. I was commissioner for the Japanese Pavilion, with the participation of photographer Ryuji Miyamoto and architects Osamu Ishiyama and Katsuhiro Miyamoto.

4. *Visions of Japan*, Victoria & Albert Museum, London, England, September 17, 1991–January 15, 1992.

5. Minamata Memorial, Minamata City, Kumamoto Prefecture, Japan, 1996. In 1995, Minamata City held a design competition for a resting place for the spirits of the victims of industrial mercury poisoning, with the hope of teaching future generations about the tragedy. The design of an Italian architect, Giuseppe Barone, was chosen from among 453 entries, and construction began in 1996.

6. Gifu Kitagata Apartments, Kitagata-cho, Gifu Prefecture, Japan, 1998. Arata Isozaki & Associates was the coordinator of the whole project; the dwelling units were designed by Kazuyo Sejima, Akiko Takahashi, Christine Hawley, and Elizabeth Diller; the courtyard by Martha Schwartz; the conference hall by Emi Fukuzawa, the public sculpture by Aiko Miyawaki.

7. *"Haishi": Mirage City–Another Utopia*, NTT Intercommunication Center, Tokyo, Japan, April 19–July 13, 1997.

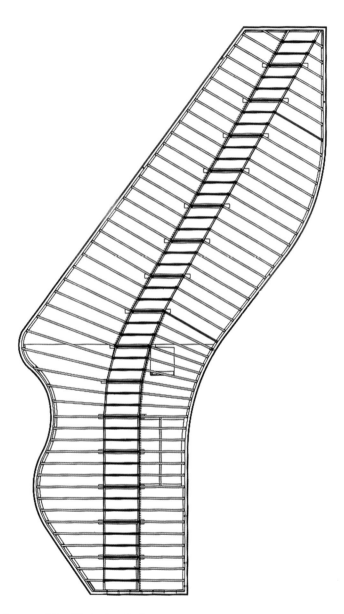

Roof plan of Japanese Art and Technology Center

JAPANESE ART AND TECHNOLOGY CENTER

Kraków, Poland, 1990–94

When Polish film director Andrzej Wajda received the Kyoto Prize in 1987, he announced a plan to construct a Center for Japanese Art and Technology in the city of Kraków, using the prize as starter money for the project. With the assistance of the governments of both countries and donations from more than 100,000 people in Japan, the center opened in November 1994.

Kraków is a historic city, with numerous medieval buildings still standing. The city provided a site across from Wawel Royal Castle on the bank of the Vistula River, which runs around the center of the city. Isozaki was given the job of designing the building. Echoing the gentle meandering path of the river, the building is composed of curvilinear shapes in both plan and elevation. Because the site is triangular, bounded by the street and a promenade along the riverbanks, the building takes an irregular shape in plan. Tracing a sine curve, the ridge of the roof also responds to the shape of the site. Brick walls form a gate-shaped space down the central axis that corresponds to the backbone of the building. Walls around the exterior of the gate are clad in locally quarried pink sandstone, with the ends linked by beams in composite material. Since the peak is also curved, the roof that links the two forms a plane bent along two axes. Above, wood lathing was attached with insulation over it, and the whole was covered in galvanized steel sheet.

The main portion of the center is an exhibition area, where *ukiyo-e* and other works of art collected by turn-of-the-century Japanologist Feliks Jasienski form the body of the permanent collection. Light enters from above the corridor of brick arches, where products of Japanese technology are displayed. The entrance is reached by a staircase and a ramp from the street in front. Behind the entrance is a reading area with reference materials on Japanese art and technology, and a cafe terrace with a view of Wawel Castle on the far bank. The basement houses storage and curators' offices, but it also contains a small multifunctional hall for all kinds of experimental theater. The Center's future plans include creating Japanese-style gardens in the front and back of the building.

Fund-raising, design, and construction of the Center took eight years. The project was slowed as it encountered the difficult period of Poland's second revolution, followed by a recession in Japan that threatened funding. Through the efforts of countless individuals, however, this project created new bonds of friendship and stimulated cultural exchange between the two countries, and was finally completed on this ideal site. The building stands as testimony to the good will of all those who participated.

General view across the Vistula River on the east side

Lobby, curving glazed wall

View of the exhibition space

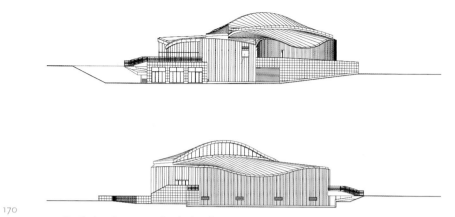

TOP **North elevation,** BOTTOM **South elevation**

View of the east side

Detail of the facing

East elevation

NAGI MUSEUM OF CONTEMPORARY ART

Nagi, Okayama, Japan, 1991–94

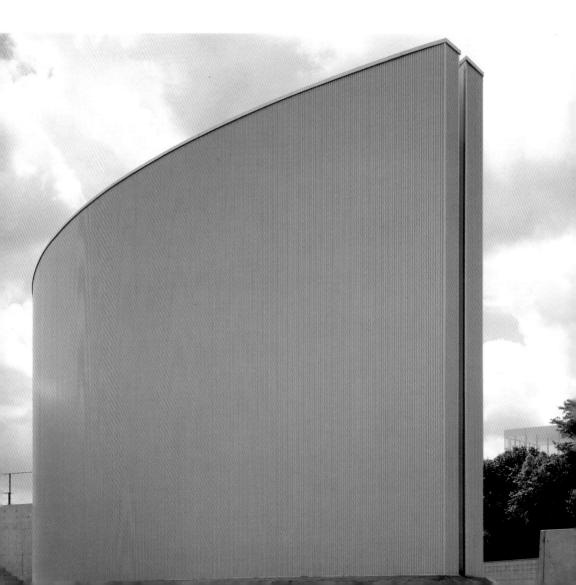

The Nagi Museum of Contemporary Art is an entirely new type of contemporary art museum. As a building type the museum has been evolving since the nineteenth century, and in content and form Nagi MOCA is what might be called a third-generation art museum.

Art museums came into being at the end of the eighteenth century as places to exhibit royal and aristocratic collections. Works of art from ancient times onward were gathered and exhibited there, with framed paintings and sculptures on pedestals. The artworks were in many cases torn from their original settings to be brought together under one roof. The Louvre, and much later on, the Tokyo National Museum offer examples of such first-generation art museums. Modern art, beginning with Impressionism, emerged in the late nineteenth century, partly in opposition to the authority of this kind of art museum.

Modernism ultimately reduced most artworks to planes and solid geometric figures. Art museums with adjustable floors and walls were best suited for exhibiting such works. The Centre Pompidou in Paris, the Museum of Modern Art in New York, and many recently designed museums of modern art in Japan are examples of second-generation art museums.

Since the 1960s, artists have continued to experiment with different forms of art, creating works that transcend the materiality of plane and solid; these often extend into the rooms in which their site-specific works are arranged. Art museums designed to exhibit such works have not hitherto existed. A museum of this kind requires the architecturalization of spaces conceived by living artists. Today, we are witnessing in fragmentary form the beginning of a trend toward third-generation art museums, so-called museums of contemporary art.

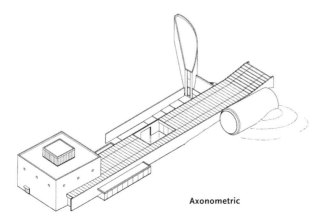

Axonometric

North view of "Moon"

What makes Nagi MOCA even more noteworthy is its location. Local governments all over Japan have been rushing to construct cultural facilities—too often, simple boxes put up without much forethought—but it is the virtually unknown town of Nagi, in Okayama Prefecture, that is giving birth to this unique project.

At Nagi MOCA, three artists—Shusaku Arakawa, Kazuo Okazaki, and Aiko Miyawaki—have been asked to create works that cannot be accommodated in conventional museum galleries. The spaces for these works have been integrated into the architecture. Each work is intended to be entered and experienced physically, but it is also clearly configured from the outside. The sun, the moon, and the earth are used as metaphors in the three works (or places).

All three are site-specific, i.e., created in situ. Since each will assimilate every element of the interior space (notably shape, light, materials, perspective, and time), viewers must visit the site and enter and experience the work to appreciate it. It is hoped that viewers will stop to contemplate these works and their meanings. Media such as photography, print, or video alone can never completely convey their complex spatial character.

The collaboration of architects and artists in the production of such site-specific works will be the only way of collecting and exhibiting them in the future. Nagi MOCA may well be the first attempt at a museum of this kind in the world. It will no doubt provide a model for architectural spaces that are adapted to the art of today and of the future. Nagi MOCA is especially important because this approach is being taken by a public museum.

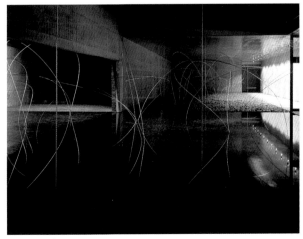

Room "Earth"
Utsurohi: A Moment of Movement by Aiko Miyawaki

Anteroom for room "Sun"

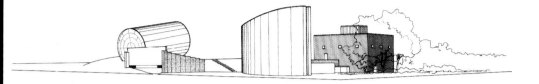

Perspective

Entrance, view from south

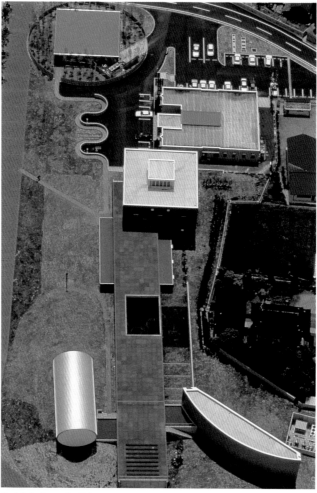

Aerial photograph of the museum

East view of "Sun"

View of museum and library from restaurant

Room "Moon": *Garden of Supplement* •
Hisashi: That Which Supplements by Kazuo Okazaki

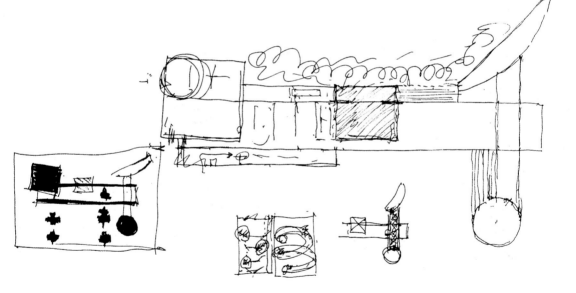

Sketch

KYOTO CONCERT HALL

Kyoto, Japan, 1991–95

Overall view from the east

Kyoto Concert Hall is the city's first music hall designed exclusively for symphony performances. It embodies Kyoto's motto of being an "International, Cultural, Free City." The hall was planned to commemorate the 1,200-year anniversary of Heian Kyo, the ancient capital and precursor of modern Kyoto.

The 9,900-square-meter site is in the Kitayama section of Kyoto, part of a larger 50,000-square-meter area to be developed in the future as a "culture plaza." The hall occupies the center of one side of a triangle between three ancient sites: Funa-oka Yama, the defining point of the central axis—true north—of Heian Kyo; Shimogamo Shrine; and Kamigamo Shrine. The Kamo River runs along the western edge of the site, the same side of the triangle as Funa-oka Yama, toward the Boar (i) direction of the twelve Chinese zodiacal signs, which indicate directions, time, and year. Kitayama Dori, the avenue that borders the north edge of the site, is shifted slightly toward magnetic north in relation to the ancient urban axis. These three axes, inherent in the urban structure of Kyoto—true north, the Boar direction, and magnetic north—have been extracted and rearranged along with three basic geometric forms: a parallelepiped, a cylinder, and a cubic grid.

The parallelepiped, completely covered with precast concrete panels blended with peridotite, contains a large, rectilinear hall. The cylinder encases an entrance hall, and a small, hexagonal auditorium is inscribed directly above it, featuring newly developed exterior ceramic plates. The cubic grid, composed of 7.8-meter units, contains the foyers for both concert auditoriums and is framed in cast aluminum. Bridging these two halls are cast aluminum louvers, set in horizontal curves, which give the impression of a low-lying mist. The colors of the surface materials, ranging from light gray to black, allow the architecture to harmonize with its surroundings while discreetly drawing attention to its forms.

The approach path is long and winds back and forth. Circulation is guided to the rear of the site, like the approach to a shrine or temple, then the path folds back on itself and finally reaches the entrance hall. It follows an ascending spiral ramp encircling the entrance hall and then the smaller hall, and arrives eventually at the foyer of the large concert hall and then that of the smaller one. This spatial sequencing seeks to build anticipation for the music as it detaches concertgoers from their daily temporal-spatial routine.

The large hall accommodates an audience of 1,839, with two tiers of balcony seats on either side of the parquet and additional seats behind the stage. In this arrangement the seats surround the stage. The lower balconies are uniform and parallel to the side walls, while the upper ones are in a staggered formation, alternately projecting and receding. Based on the classical rectangular type of concert hall, the Kyoto hall also makes use of the "vineyard" type of continuous floor rise, a new development in this century, in which seats are arranged on irregular terraced floors.

A ninety-stop pipe organ is set off-center to the geometry of the seating; this placement softens the powerful axial centrality of the hall while answering the asymmetry of the orchestra itself. For the sake of acoustics, various concave-convex architectonic elements are introduced. The 1,500 small protrusions on the ceiling effectively reflect and diffuse sound while creating a band of light that sparkles like the Milky Way—an effect of the recessed lighting. The stage can easily accommodate a full orchestra in addition to a 100-member chorus, and is equipped with an elevating mechanism that can modulate its height by as much as 1,200 millimeters. The podium seats at the rear of the stage can be transformed into risers by folding down the backs, thereby extending the stage.

The small concert hall seats an audience of 514. This space, inscribed in a cylindrical drum, is for chamber music. The particular form, opening upward, was achieved by taking advantage of the gap between the lowered ceiling and the legally restricted full height of the structure. The primary material of the slanted walls is 3-millimeter-thick punched aluminum, which is acoustically transparent, so the actual reflective surface is hidden behind it. Installed on the dark colored ceiling are large and small lighting fixtures called "UFOs," which can be moved up and down.

The entrance hall, situated beneath the chamber music hall, is an unusual space, surrounded by the space's canted envelope and the upward spiraling ramp. Twelve post-like exhaust cylinders (inscribed with zodiacal signs) for air circulation and a bronze Chinese-style compass inlaid in the center of the marble floor recall the azimuth, the primary tool used in the siting of the building.

In contrast to the other spaces, the foyer is bright and open; in the tradition of Japanese gardens, it uses borrowed landscapes (*shakkei*) from the adjacent Kyoto City Botanical Garden and the mountain ranges to the west of the city. The cubic grid is covered with *pietra serena* (Florentine limestone), and a semitransparent glass screen softens the direct sunlight across the fenestration of the foyer.

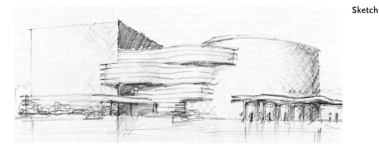

Sketch

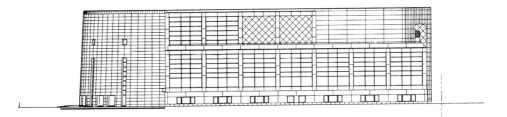

West elevation

Foyer of small hall

KYOTO CONCERT HALL

Ceiling of small hall

Entrance side facade

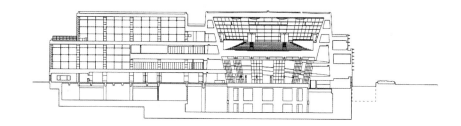

190

Large hall

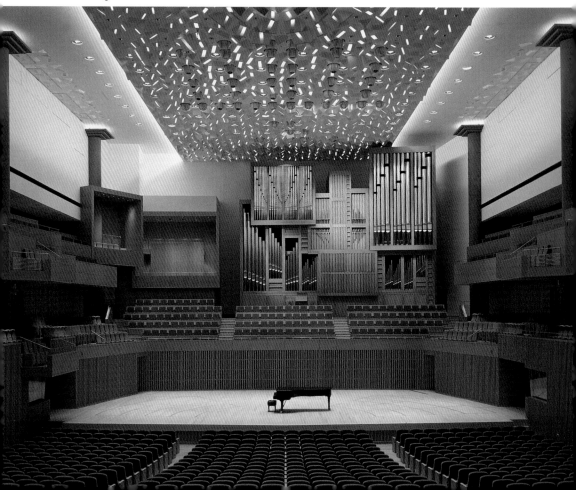

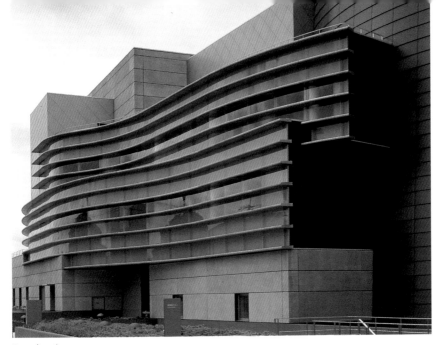

East elevation

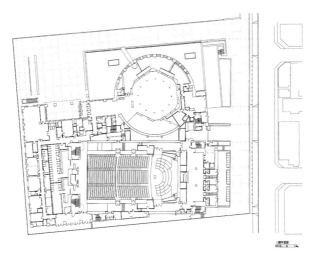

First-floor plan

TOYONOKUNI LIBRARIES FOR CULTURAL RESOURCES

Oita, Japan, 1991–95

Ceiling of the "space of one hundred columns"

Nearly thirty years have passed since the opening of Isozaki's Oita Prefectural Library building in 1966. The number of books have long since exceeded capacity. At the same time the computerization of the library holdings has been a concern in recent years.

This new plan called for a multiuse assembly combining a prefectural library, a public archive, and a "wise-man's resource center" on an approximately 15,000-square-meter site. The capacity of the new library is 1.6 million books, about four times that of the old structure. The 4,500-square-meter open-stack reading room, with 300 seats and 300,000 books, is presently the largest in Japan. The space consists of an 81-unit grid of steel-reinforced-concrete "cubes" without structural walls—an array of 7.5-cubic-meter units and 100 vertical columns. Ventilation and lighting are maintained as homogeneously as possible throughout the grid, while natural light filters down through regularly placed skylights.

This homogeneous grid can accommodate movement of partitions, increased computerization, and changes in shelf arrangement, all of which must be anticipated in a contemporary library. The "one-hundred-column space" is a prototype for public libraries that need not dictate the position of bookshelves, desks, computer terminals, people, or information. Such an arrangement facilitates all conceivable alterations, as well as those not yet imagined.

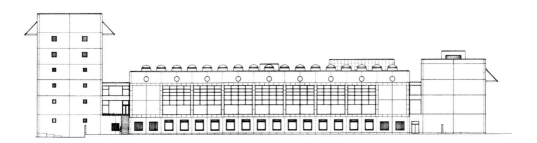

North elevation

View from south

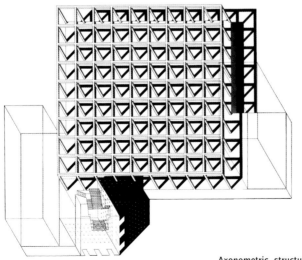

Axonometric, structural system

View toward entrance

Stairs to the "space of one hundred columns"

Interior of the entrance hall

OKAYAMA WEST POLICE STATION

Okayama, Japan, 1993–96

West elevation

This police station is divided into two separate blocks. The back part, clad in galvanized metal sheets, houses offices and holding cells. The front, equal in size, is further divided into two sections, east and west. The east section, facing a granite-paved plaza, consists only of slender steel columns; it can be seen as a porch, or an extension of the plaza within the building. The west section is primarily of glass, with precast granite-faced panels arranged in a checkerboard pattern. This repeats the bipartite pattern of division, but creates an oblique emphasis. The facilities of the west section are open to the public. They include training rooms for judo, karate, and kendo; the traffic department; and a conference space. The floor heights vary, and the checkerboard pattern is repeated on the floor surfaces. Finally, a translucent sunscreen serves as transition from the portico.

Dividing this structure into two parts determines its outline, but this is not the expression of an arbitrary compositional idea. The gesture reflects the internal organization of the building, while conserving, at the same time, a certain ambiguity, as the partitioning is not just binary. If each of the parts had been treated in a uniform manner, with a single material, the dichotomy would have been absolute. The aim of the design, however, was to avoid such simplicity. It is the ambiguity of this gesture—unambiguous in itself—that shifts the outline of the building envelope.

The wall clad in zinc sheets conceals the inner volume, while dematerializing it into a surface of vertically repeated elements. Columns of steel pipe reduced to a minimum diameter, standing together, transform the eastern section of the facade into a kind of forest. The checkerboard pattern disrupts the homogeneity of the elevation and varies the regular design of the glazing. All materials used fully declare their own nature—they were chosen to endow the facade as pure texture. Nevertheless, texture addresses substance; but because it is not divided and requires no articulation, it is noncompositional. In this building, outlines are ambiguous while surface materials are not; they candidly display their own quality. This accurately reflects the objective significance of materials today, their resistance to the mirage of the landscape of virtual reality. In this work, the division of things into two parts is intended to reveal that suspended instant in which material becomes reality.

Overall view from southeast

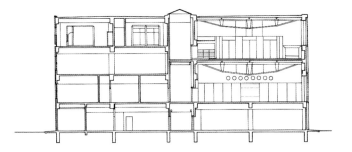

North–south section

Columns of the portico

View from south

Interior of tatami training room

The upper part of the lobby

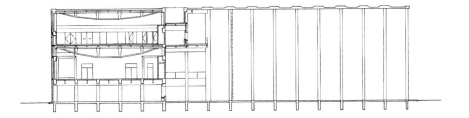

West–east section

Detail of the paving and the columns of the portico

View from the north

NARA CONVENTION HALL

Nara, Japan, 1992–

Computer graphic, overall view from the east

SITE

Nara was Japan's capital for much of the eighth century. The Japanese name for Japan, Nihon, was coined around the end of the seventh century, and Nara was the first capital to promote this name. The style of Japan's new capital was almost totally that of the Sui dynasty capitals in China (A.D. 581–618): a grid based on the north-south axis was applied to the main area, and the imperial palace was placed at the north-central edge of the grid. A number of large temples were constructed in and around the grid; most of them have burned down, but a few have been restored, including Todai-ji Temple, the largest wooden structure in the world. When the capital was later moved to Kyoto, Nara's urban life gradually declined. Now the city is a famous tourist site and the government center for the region.

Today the city's original grid remains almost untouched, except for certain areas destroyed when the railroad was introduced without regard for ancient streets and buildings. When redevelopment of the area next to Nara station was announced, the architect Kisho Kurokawa came up with a master plan that set aside one sector as a kind of architectural exposition, and his idea was accepted. As the nation's economy was thriving,

groundbreaking for the project began immediately, although construction has slowed since the economy weakened in the early 1990s.

On the site of the Nara Convention Hall, the western and northern edges follow the city's ancient grid, while the southern and eastern edges describe an angle bordered by the streets haphazardly created by the railroad's intrusion. The scheme proposed by Isozaki is an ellipsoid oriented along the traditional north-south grid, while an entrance wall opens toward pedestrians who arrive from the Nara train station via a pedestrian bridge.

PROGRAM

In 1991, an international competition for the convention center was organized as a part of the Nara Architectural Exposition. A total of 2,918 proposals were submitted, from which five semifinalists were chosen: Bojan Radonic & Goran Rako; Yoshito Takahashi; Bahram Shirdel & Robert Livesey; Ryuji Nakamura/Takenaka Corporation; and Scott Marble & Karen Fairbank. In addition, schemes were commissioned from Tadao Ando, Mario Botta, Hans Hollein, Isozaki, and Christian de Portzamparc. The final plan for the convention center illustrated was selected from these ten. The jurors were Kurokawa (principal juror), Kazuo Shinohara, Hiroshi Hara, the late James Stirling, Richard Meier, Vittorio Lampugnani, Makoto Ohgita (chair of the Urban Landscape Council of Nara City), Eizo Nishida (mayor of Nara City), and Kiyokazu Asakawa (chair of the Nara City Assembly).

The project brief included a convention hall to accommodate 1,800 people; a midsize concert hall to accommodate 500; and the support spaces for these two halls. At the outset of the project, a large underground parking area and HVAC plant for the facility were to be included in the program, but were later eliminated.

PARTI

The placement of architectural elements is based on Isozaki's interpretation of the specific character of Nara's urban space. When one compares the three capitals of different historical eras—Nara, Kyoto, and Tokyo—one notes a dramatic variation in the way architecture is perceived in a given urban context. Architectural contours vary with the nature of each city: Nara is characterized by its individual buildings, Kyoto by distinctive exterior spaces such as narrow paths and gardens, and Tokyo by interior spaces such as underground shopping districts, atriums, and the chasms between tall buildings.

As such, in Nara it is appropriate to plan an architectural structure as an independent monolith, as exemplified by many old temples. Thus, in this scheme the two auditoriums are assembled back to back and enclosed as a single entity. For visitors who approach from the station, one wall is "split open" to form an entrance.

In the same way that cupolas made the skylines of many European cities, the skyline of Nara is defined by the roofs of its temples. These roofs, as well as those of surrounding residences, are all of dark gray tile. They suggest an expanse of ocean in which the layers of tiles are like small waves, while the curved roof silhouettes are like large swells. This perhaps explains why the four roof ornaments on top of the Great Buddha Hall at Todai-ji Temple are reminiscent of fish tails.

The outside walls of Isozaki's building are covered with newly fired tile of the same dark gray color as the ancient roofs. The form of the main outer structure is a rotated ellipsoid or clothoid curve. This has a camber, yet is consistent with the old temples' features. The scale and volume of the proposed building have been measured in relation to that of the Great Buddha Hall of Todai-ji Temple. First built some 1,300 years ago, Todai-ji Temple was twice destroyed by fire and rebuilt. When first reconstructed in the twelfth century, the interior space was tremendously large—more than twice the present structure (rebuilt in the seventeenth century with a volume of 50 cubic meters). The projected scale of the Nara Convention Hall is larger than the present Todai-ji Temple, but smaller than its original.

Against its background of low surrounding houses, the structure looks as if a giant Buddha had graced the site. Scenes with a comparable dramatic flair have been depicted in many paintings of "The Descent of Buddha Amitabha." These representations sought to visualize an apparition of the transcendent; and by its dramatic differentiation of form and scale from the surrounding houses, this design sought a monumental symbol for the hundredth anniversary of Nara's municipal government.

A VARIABLE THEATER

At the earliest phase of the competition, the Isozaki design team proposed to construct a theater with a movable stage that could vary its relationship with the audience and accommodate different uses. It would have shifted from a proscenium stage to theater in the round through a combination of rotation and a shift of audience seats. In the final design phase, other technical options were proposed for altering the relationship between stage (taking what is not visible into account as well) and audience.

As a result, three functions will be included: a shallow stage for lectures, symposia, film projections, and the like; a deep stage with wings for theater performances; and an arena stage for Sumo wrestling, boxing, and the like. Furthermore, Isozaki proposed using the space behind the audience seats as an additional part of the stage—an "imaginary stage." To accomplish the transformation from one function to another, three moving parts were designed: a proscenium that is moved back and forth to extend or contract the stage; a trap in the ground

Sketch, studies for section, plan, and volume

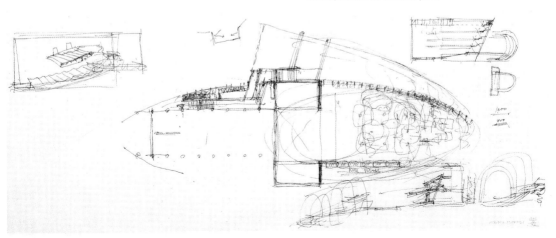

floor under the seats so that some of these are stored under the floor when the stage is changed into an arena; and last, units of audience seats at a mezzanine level that are moved to correspond to the stage's particular transformation.

A TRANSPARENT CONCERT HALL

The midsize, 500-person concert hall is designed to enhance acoustical effects for small orchestras and chamber music groups. This occupies the second floor of the building, while offices and backstage functions are accommodated below.

The interior of the rotated ellipsoid is to receive a smooth concrete finish; two glass walls are set within it, encasing a box-shaped hall between them. To diffuse the echo, the ceiling has a subtly hanging curve textured like netting, the recesses of which hide lighting fixtures and absorb sound.

The inside surfaces of the double glass partition walls are randomly angled as part of the overall acoustics design. The space between the glass box and the external shell contains a foyer and cafe, through which one can survey the features of the entire space, with sunlight streaming through the glass.

INSIDE AND/OR OUTSIDE

A neutral space—neither interior nor exterior—has been created by turning a part of the

Computer graphic, interior of the small hall

rotating ellipsoid wall at an angle to the enclosed auditorium to form a large, free-standing surface. This new wall is made of the same composite material as the main enclosure, and both walls are structurally connected to the skylit roof. The wider end of this ellipsoid-shaped atrium serves as the entrance from the train station. The space thus created, which faces the pedestrian platform access toward the station, has broad steps that can double as audience seats. A terrace in front of the entrance becomes an outside stage.

STRUCTURAL CONCEPT

A traditional Japanese wooden bucket is assembled by making a ring of separate slats and fastening them with strips of steel. This kind of structure is possible as long as the base is a single board. Suppose we overturn the bucket and make the circle elliptical, turn the base into a roof, and connect the separate boards with hidden joints. If the boards are replaced by 3 x 25-meter slabs of precast concrete and reinforced with steel plate, we have the structure of Nara Convention Hall: major axis 135 meters, minor axis 42 meters, and height 25 meters.

The structure of the bucket is like that of a ship. Turning it upside down gives it the basic requirements of architecture. In the actual design process, the thrust of the metaphor was the other way around. First came the rotated ellipsoid—the final shape of the monolith. Size was determined by the

desired capacity of the auditorium. Once the sleek surface was chosen, Isozaki's design team began to think of the support structure's continuous contour as a kind of shell. Giving it a supporting keel connects it metaphorically with a ship. In fact, during the competition one of the judges compared its form to that of a nuclear submarine. But the Isozaki team wanted to reduce the number of internal walls, so first they conceived the outer block, dividing the unit to facilitate circulation. Had they chosen the keel structure, they would have been obliged structurally to divide the space into more than two parts. Finally, they decided to replace the keel with panels of precast concrete. Thus came the metaphor of the bucket for the structural body. By turning the whole unit into a ring, the structure suddenly becomes lighter. Professor Mamoru Kawaguchi refers to this structure as the "dome effect."

Inside the thin outer blocks is a separate wall that cuts through the middle of the ellipsoid, across the back of each auditorium.

"PANTA-UP"

In December 1997, over a six-day period, the outside panels of the ellipsoid, which had been positioned jacknife-fashion on the ground, were unfolded and fixed to a height of 25 meters from ground level. To accommodate delivery and construction, the panels had been assembled in two parts and hinged. Meanwhile, separate hinges were used to fix them at ground and roof level. It was as if the folded structure had suddenly risen from a squatting position. This construction method, called "Panta-Up," invented and patented by Kawaguchi, had previously been used by Isozaki at the Sant Jordi Sports Hall, but only for a steel skeleton. One important feature of the method is that it enables a large span roof to be erected without the need for internal scaffolding. In this construction method, the concrete roofing plates as well as the inner ceiling and suspended devices that house the mechanical equipment for the theater were all constructed on

the ground and then raised; altogether, they weighed approximately 4,600 tons.

In Japan, the raising of a roof structure is traditionally called *mune age*, and ritual is part of the occasion. Nara city celebrated the erection of the Nara Convention Hall roof as a new ritual. It corresponds to the Western rites celebrating the erection of cupolas.

In less than a week, the huge features of something resembling a starship had appeared behind the neighboring residences. At the beginning, when the walls of the shell were still folded, it looked like a huge

Panta-Dome construction method

insect. Later it gradually metamorphosed to a chrysalis, and then came the final stage. For Isozaki, this process of metamorphosis epitomizes the design and was its principal feature.

At Nara, Isozaki made use of scarcely any traditional compositional methods or construction methods. Perhaps as a result, the convention hall is merely object-like. But Isozaki believes that it can be called "architecture." When the building is completed, it will be sandwiched between works by Rossi and Kurokawa—postmodern works that incorporate historical elements in different ways. Isozaki predicts that the effect will be quite strange, deviating as it must from architectural conventions; for this reason, he believes that it can be called architecture on a deeper level.

Since the roof was raised, interior finish and exterior facing have proceeded, and the whole project is due to be complete by the end of 1998. The public opening will take place in February 1999, one hundred years after Nara became a modern municipality, and thirteen centuries after its original foundation.

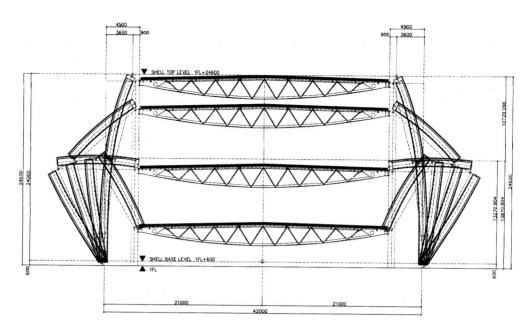

Cross-section of the structure, with the different assembly phases

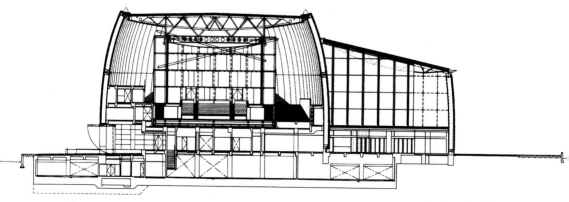

East–west section

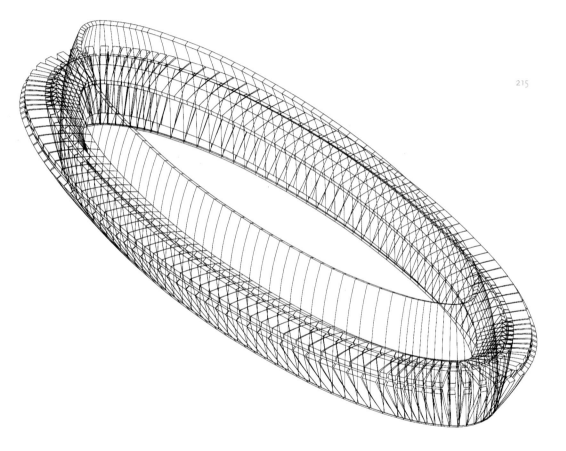

Panta-up construction, scheme

Model, overall view from north

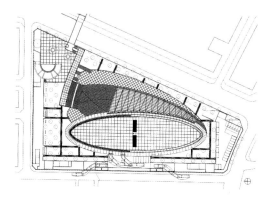

Site plan

Computer graphic, entrance space

DOMUS: INTERACTIVE MUSEUM ABOUT HUMANS

La Coruña, Spain, 1993–95

This museum, overlooking Orzán Bay, is distinctive in its topographic, climatic, cultural, and urban qualities. The principal function of Domus is to allow visitors to experience the many aspects of human body mechanism through an interactive system of exhibits. Its spatial configuration results from an interpretation of these contexts in search of an architectural equivalent.

The site is atop a steeply rising cliff facing out over the sea. The city of La Coruña constructed a long promenade along the shore of this peninsula, jutting seaward between two bays. The entry level of the museum is 17 meters above the promenade, which is itself 20 meters from the shoreline. Domus is linked to the promenade by a grand stairway. Terraces are inserted as rest places along this approach with a scenic backdrop of La Coruña.

La Coruña has been a seaport since ancient times; a lighthouse, an important landmark, was built here during the Roman era. (It stands today as it has since the eighteenth century when it was restored using a neoclassicist vocabulary.) From the opposite shore, it is clear that the peninsula is being developed as an urban area. However, the museum site—once a quarry—was left intact by sheer chance, perhaps because it was too difficult to build on. Situating a single building here requires the architect to surpass the scale of the residential backdrop in order to achieve a distinct imagery in scale with the Roman lighthouse. A simple form was needed to make a clear impression from far away.

The Galician region of northwestern Spain is known for the fierce wind that blows from the ocean and the rough waves it creates. Orzán Bay, being an inlet, is relatively calm, but the outer shores of this peninsula are sometimes battered by rough waves and subject to fierce rain. This severe climate calls for a solid building. Facing the sea, Isozaki created a curving barrier wall that looks as if it has been shaped by the wind. Since the interior is mostly exhibition space, large openings in this wall were not needed. The wall consists of a series of 2.6-meter precast-concrete units assembled to create a 94-meter wall, 17 meters high. Its surface is waterproofed, insulated, and covered in green slate panels 3 centimeters thick. The concrete wall's interior surface is left exposed. Since the rear of the museum faces a residential area, zigzag walls resembling a Japanese folding screen were designed to afford a pedestrian scale. These screen elements have an average height of 11 meters and were constructed directly upon the living rock. Made of 5.5-centimeter-thick granite panel backed by concrete, the walls are of minimal thickness to resist the wind from the ocean. The roof, part of which consists of one long skylight, is stabilized by a simple

View from the north

drop truss and spans the area between these two walls of totally different character.

Impermeable to wind and weather, the barrier wall is a kind of mask and, as such, scarcely reflects the content of the museum's exhibitions. Yet despite its masking quality, it is hoped that the wall will express the character of the facility in the same way that the skin hides the mysteries of the human body. In plan the wall is an arc, but volumetrically it becomes a clothoid curve, hydrodynamic in character.

Isozaki set out to achieve a new sense of lightness not normally created with stone. Throughout the project, only rock from the Galician region was used.

From the promenade along the shore, visitors to the museum mount a grand stairway and, just past the first corner of the building, encounter an approach carved from the rock itself. Here is the entrance. The interior is a single continuous exhibition space

on three levels, connected by a circulation ramp that follows the contours of the rocky topography. The exhibition space, from floors to handrails, is faced in slate. Placed throughout are interactive exhibits, illuminated by soft natural light entering only from above.

An auditorium for film projection and other visual media is located at the end of the circulation route; it can also be used for lectures and conferences. The museum offices are above.

In addition, the museum has a restaurant, below the exhibition area, with its own entrance. Only here was the view an important consideration. Thus, the wall facing the sea—and expanded by a terrace—is of continuous framed glazing in the tradition of Spain's northern coast.

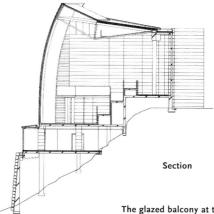

Section

**The glazed balcony at the restaurant is a "glass gallery,"
a traditional feature in La Coruña**

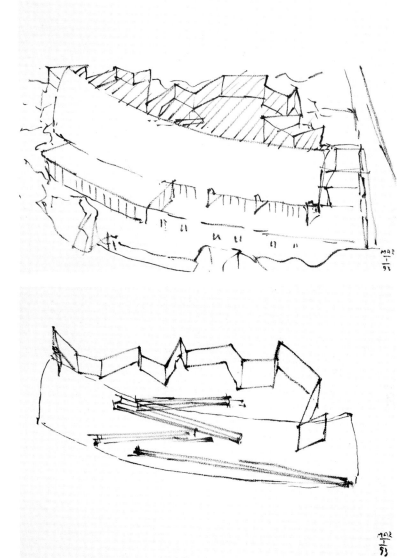

Sketches

View from east

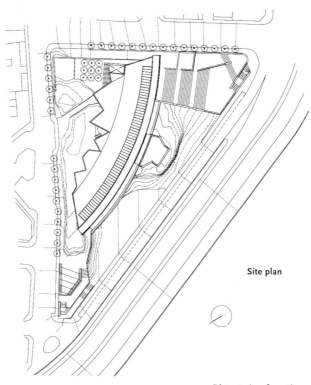

Site plan

Distant view from the south across the bay

South facade. The exterior wall is clad in green slate panels.

View of the exhibition space

CENTER OF SCIENCE AND INDUSTRY (COSI)

Columbus, Ohio, 1994–

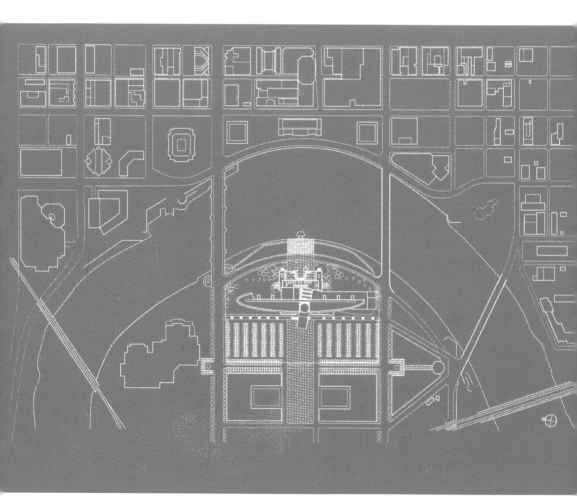

Site plan

The Center of Science and Industry (COSI) enjoys a monumental site on the tip of a peninsula across the river and one city block from the statehouse square in downtown Columbus, Ohio. An existing city planning axis aligns this site with the statehouse square and city hall. A former high school building, an example of midwestern academic classicism, occupies this prominent axis, facing east toward the river and downtown. This building was designated for preservation and incorporated into the project.

To clarify its position within the city, the COSI building is designed almost symmetrically to embrace the former high school building astride the city axis. Given the context, Isozaki considers this the last monumental site in the city. The east facade of the old high school has been kept intact, as a formal entrance to the complex facing the city. To the west, the city fabric becomes less rigid so that a radically different treatment was chosen for the west façade. An analogy was drawn between this facade and the orientation of the frontier in American history. An elliptical masklike wall will confront the "wild west." Its form is a vast, hydrodynamic surface that transcends the usual scale of building to proclaim the site's monumentality and urban scale.

The entire complex is planned as a science museum that will feature an educational program intended to complement the neighboring schools' curriculum. Its program is designed to anticipate continual changes in technology. The building is conceived in three parts: the former high school houses educational facilities. The elliptical section will contain the exhibition program and is flexibly structured. The additional platonic forms, such as cylinders and cubes, comprise the fixed elements of theater and atrium. Therefore, the building becomes a huge shelter to house these changing contents, a sort of scientific theme park at a large scale.

The building has been under construction since early 1997, and completion is anticipated in fall 1999.

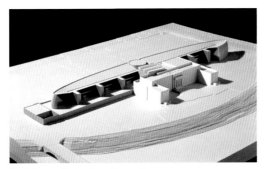

Model, overall view from the east

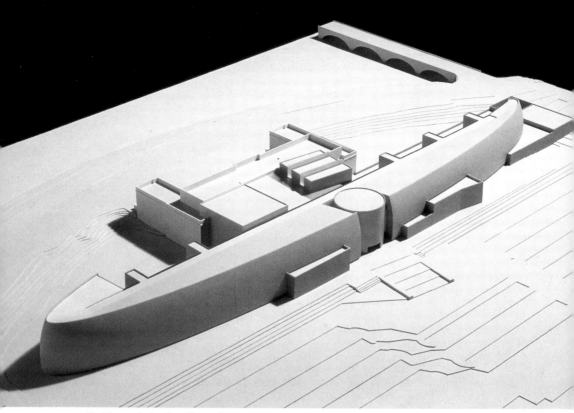

Model, overall view from the south

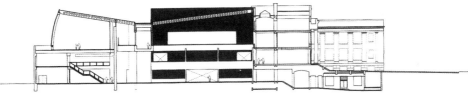

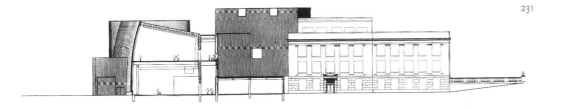

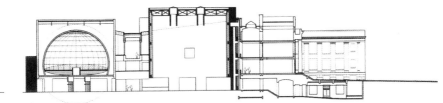

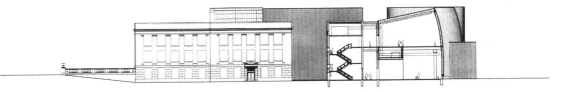

Section drawings: TOP center axis; SECOND south wing; atrium-space theater; BOTTOM north wing

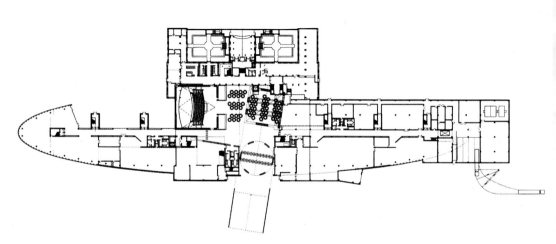

Plan, 720 feet above sea level

Two sketches

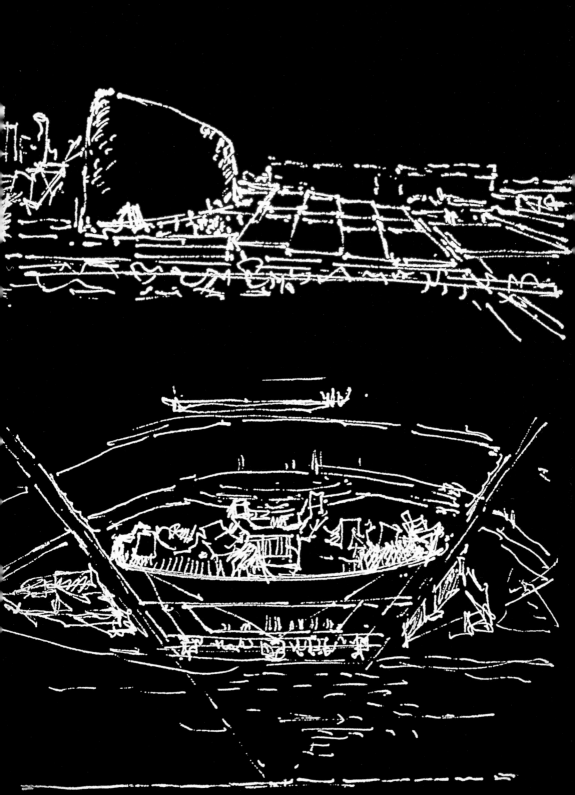

CONCEPTUAL PROPOSAL: Mirage City

South China Sea, 1994–

One of the current projects in Isozaki's studio is a design proposal for an artificial island off Macao in the South China Sea, commissioned by the municipal government of Zhuhai City. It is referred to as Haishi Jimua.

There are double implications in the term haishi: its literal meaning is "city on the sea," but it also implies a mirage. Now that the municipal government is seriously considering this project and the sponsors are researching its economic and technical aspects, it is not entirely certain whether the project will be a city or a mirage. In any event, it is possible to see this project as a utopia, because a city on the sea evokes a world totally detached from contemporary political institutions and social conventions.

It has been approximately one half-century since the death of many kinds of utopias, yet they are still fresh in our minds. What does it mean to project another utopia, before these others have completely disappeared? The question of whether to consider the new utopia as a ritual of revival, a repetitive farce, or a new vision of emancipation makes the

Computer graphic, first version

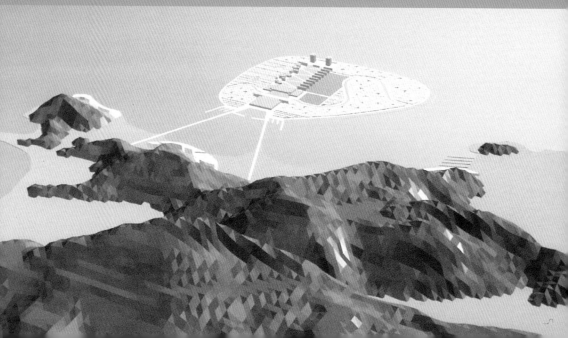

position of those contemplating it today totally different from what preceded it. Furthermore, the realization of this project must involve all possible points of view. The notion of producing a project can no longer take linear relations for granted: projects no longer progress diachronically through posturing but unfold only as a negotiation among different positions.

It is interesting that Sir Thomas More—who was among the first to write about a utopia, in his 1516 book of that name (which he coined)—sited Nowhere Land on an island that would be discovered only after a long ocean voyage. The artificial island of this project will also appear in the sea, but whereas the former was envisioned in an age in which frontiers still held real expectations of new discovery, the latter is a fictive construct placed on a sea where there is seemingly nothing left to discover. The first edition of More's *Utopia* contained an illustration of the island, which in the second edition (1518) was changed by the addition of two bridges that connected the island to the shore of Somewhere Land. Why More made this change is unknown. In any case, the topographical conditions of More's illustrated island are quite similar to those of the Mirage City island. The city of Venice, today connected to the mainland by a long bridge, and the second edition of *Utopia* provided the inspiration to connect the Mirage City island to maintain China with two bridges.

Four fundamental axes: feng-shui, Chinese geomency, was used as a reference to determine the gestalt of the artificial island

Panel: Sixth International Architecture Exhibition, Venice Biennale (left and right)

HAISHI AS MIRAGE CITY (1994–) IS THE CONSTRUCTION OF AN ARTIFICIAL ISLAND IN THE MIDST OF THE SOUTH CHINA SEA OFF MACAO. THE ORIGINAL CONCEPTUALIZATION BEGAN AT THE REQUEST OF THE GOVERNMENT OF ZHUHAI CITY, THE MUNICIPALITY WITH WHICH MACAO WILL MERGE IN 1999.

THE ISLAND IS LOCATED AT THE CROSSROADS OF EAST/WEST AND PAST/FUTURE, WHERE THE FLOW OF *qi* SPRINGS UP THROUGH THE DRAGON VEIN ORIGINATING IN THE SACRED MOUNTAIN. IT LOOKS LIKE A MIRAGE FLOATING IN THE SEA, SOMETHING LIKE WHAT SIR THOMAS MORE DESCRIBED IN HIS BOOK, *Utopia*.

THE COMMUNITY STRUCTURE OF *HAISHI* TRANSGRESSES CONVENTIONAL POLITICAL, ECONOMICAL AND SOCIAL INSTITUTIONS AND SUPPORTS THE FUNDAMENTAL SHIFT IN LIFESTYLE HABITS THAT WILL BE NECESSITATED BY THE INTRODUCTION OF MANY KINDS OF ALTERNATIVE TECHNOLOGIES—FROM NEW CONSTRUCTION METHODS TO ENERGY EFFICIENT POWER SOURCES, TRANSPORTATION SYSTEMS AND THE RAPIDLY CHANGING COMMUNICATION MEDIA.

Left panel: one set, six pieces

... A MODEL OF THE NEW WORLD WHICH HAS BEEN EMERGING EVER SINCE THE DISAPPEARANCE OF THE THREE CONCEPTUAL BASES FOR MODERNITY: THE FRONTIER—WHICH IT WAS POSSIBLE TO BELIEVE IN ONLY WHEN ONE'S TERRITORY WAS INFINITLY EXPANDABLE; THE BOUNDARAY—WHICH EXISTED WHEN MULTIPLE NATION-STATES GUARDED THEIR OWN DOMAINS IN TENSION WITH OTHERS; AND THE VANISHING POINT—WHICH STABILIZED THE ORIGIN OF THE GAZE OF MODERN SUBJECTIVITY.

A CENTRAL ORGANIZATION OF THE POLITICAL COMMUNITIES OF ASIA MAY COME TOGETHER SOONER OR LATER, JUST AS THE EUROPEAN NATIONS HAVE FORMED A UNION. *HAISHI*, AS MIRAGE CITY, WILL MAKE AN IDEAL CENTER FOR THESE ACTIVITIES IN SHARP CONTRAST TO THE MODERN CONVENTION THAT THE MAIN REQUISITE FOR POWER IS TO RULE THE SURFACE OF THE LAND.

BUISINESS FACILITIES EQUIPPED WITH A NEW INFORMATION NETWORK WILL BE CREATED. THE INFORMATION HIGHWAY AND SATELLITES WHICH ARE NOW TRANSFORMING ALL THE INSTITUTIONS OF OUR SOCIAL ACTIVITIES DECOMPOSE THE ELEMENTS OF OUR DAILY WORLD INTO BITS AND RECONSTRUCT THEM INTO DIGITAL INFORMATICS.

All drawings, sketches, and computer graphics in this book appear courtesy of the offices of Arata Isozaki & Associates. The photographs appear courtesy of the photographers, as noted below.

SHINJUKU PROJECT
p. 29, no. 3: © Osamu Murai

OITA PREFECTURAL LIBRARY
All photos © Yasuhiro Ishimoto

FUKUOKA CITY BANK HEAD OFFICE
All photos © Yasuhiro Ishimoto

N HOUSE
All photos © Yukio Futagawa

A HOUSE
p. 53, no. 1: © Shokokusha
p. 54, no. 4: © Yasuhiro Ishimoto

YANO HOUSE
p. 57, nos. 1, 2: © Yasuhiro Ishimoto
p. 58, no. 6: © Yasuhiro Ishimoto

AOKI HOUSE
p. 61, no. 3: © Shuji Yamada

BJÖRNSON STUDIO
p. 62, nos. 1, 2: © Katsuaki Furudate

FESTIVAL PLAZA, EXPO '70
p. 64: ©Shinkenchiku
p. 66 (bottom): © Seiji Otsuji

COMPUTER-AIDED CITY
p. 67, no. 3: © Shigeo Okamoto/Shokokusha
p. 67, no. 4: © Shigeo Okamoto

THE PALLADIUM CLUB
All photos © Katsuaki Furudate

THE MUSEUM OF MODERN ART, GUNMA
All photos © Yasuhiro Ishimoto

SHUKO-SHA BUILDING
p. 79, no. 1: © Yasuhiro Ishimoto
p. 79, no. 2: © Yasuhiro Ishimoto
p. 80, no. 4: © Yasuhiro Ishimoto
p. 80, no. 5: © Kuniharu Sakumoto

THE MUSEUM OF MODERN ART, GUNMA,
CONTEMPORARY ART WING
p. 83, nos. 1, 2, 3: © Japan Architect

THE MUSEUM OF MODERN ART, GUNMA,
HIGH-DEFINITION TELEVISION THEATER,
CAFE
p. 84, nos. 1, 2: © Yasuhiro Ishimoto

KITA-KYUSHU CITY MUSEUM OF ART
p. 86: © Yasuhiro Ishimoto
p. 88: © Tomio Ohashi

ART TOWER MITO
All photos © Yasuhiro Ishimoto

THE MUSEUM OF CONTEMPORARY ART,
LOS ANGELES
p. 130: © Yasuhiro Ishimoto
p. 132: © Yasuhiro Ishimoto
p. 135: © Katsuaki Furudate
p. 136: © Yasuhiro Ishimoto
p. 137: © Yasuhiro Ishimoto
p. 138: © Yasuhiro Ishimoto
p. 139: © Katsuaki Furudate

HARA MUSEUM ARC
p. 133, nos. 1, 2: Yasuhiro Ishimoto
p. 134, nos. 4, 5: Yasuhiro Ishimoto

SANT JORDI SPORTS HALL
p. 140: © Hisao Suzuki
p. 142: © Yasuhiro Ishimoto
p. 143: © Yasuhiro Ishimoto
p. 144: © Yasuhiro Ishimoto
p. 145: © Yasuhiro Ishimoto

TEAM DISNEY BUILDING
All photos © Yasuhiro Ishimoto

NEW TOKYO CITY HALL
p. 152: © Yoshio Takase (GA photographers)
p. 153 (top): © Yoshio Takase (GA
    photographers)

JR UENO RAILWAY STATION REDEVELOPMENT
p. 156, no. 1: © Yasuhiro Ishimoto
p. 156, no. 2: © Yoshio Takase (GA
    photographers)
p. 157, no. 4: © Yasuhiro Ishimoto

JAPANESE ART AND TECHNOLOGY CENTER
All photos © Katsuaki Furudate

NAGI MUSEUM OF CONTEMPORARY ART
p. 174: © Katsuaki Furudate
p. 176: © Katsuaki Furudate

p. 177: © Katsuaki Furudate
p. 178: © Katsuaki Furudate
p. 179: © Katsuaki Furudate
p. 180 (top): © Mitsumasa Fujitsuka
p. 180 (bottom): © Katsuaki Furudate
p. 181: © Katsuaki Furudate
p. 182: © Kazuo Okazaki

KYOTO CONCERT HALL
All photos © Katsuaki Furudate

TOYONOKUNI LIBRARIES FOR CULTURAL
RESOURCES
All photos © Shinkenchiku-sha

OKAYAMA WEST POLICE STATION
p. 198: © Hisao Suzuki
p. 200: © Hisao Suzuki
p. 201: © Hisao Suzuki
p. 202 (top): © Mitsumasa Fujitsuka
p. 202 (bottom): © Hisao Suzuki
p. 203: © Mitsumasa Fujitsuka
p. 204: © Mitsumasa Fujitsuka
p. 205: © Mitsumasa Fujitsuka

NARA CONVENTION HALL
p. 212–13: © Hisao Suzuki
p. 216: © Yoshio Takase (GA photographers)

DOMUS
p. 218: © Hisao Suzuki
p. 221: © Katsuaki Furudate
p. 222: © Katsuaki Furudate
p. 224: © Katsuaki Furudate
p. 225: © Katsuaki Furudate
p. 226: © Katsuaki Furudate
p. 227: © Katsuaki Furudate

CENTER OF SCIENCE AND INDUSTRY
p. 230: © Yoshio Takase (GA photographers)
p. 231: © Yoshio Takase (GA photographers)